# More Advance Praise for *It's a Helluva Town*

"The J.M. Kaplan Fund has brought about remarkable progress in safeguarding the environment, advancing historic preservation, protecting civil liberties, and publishing in the public interest; at the center of all this good work for decades has been Joan Davidson—a trail-blazer in these areas and a graceful American hero."

—John H. Adams, Founding Director,
Natural Resources Defense Council

"By funding great ideas—and fighting for them—the Kaplan Fund for 75 years has supported urban transformations that stretch from Times Square across New York and beyond. Today, mayors from around the world tell me they want to replicate the programs and the vision that the Kaplans have helped support."

—Janette Sadik-Khan, Principal, Bloomberg Associates, and
former Commissioner, NYC Department of Transportation

"Scratch the surface of so many of the initiatives and ideas that have made New York a better place to live and work and you'll find the deft hand of the J.M. Kaplan Fund. A nimble, risk taking foundation, with a talent-scout eye for emerging leadership and a keen nose for what New York needs, its seed money and early validation of new ideas have fueled social innovation before that term was coined. Again New York owes much to a wise, energetic, and committed woman, in this case the Fund's indomitable leader for many of its 75 years, Joan K. Davidson."

—Darren Walker, President, Ford Foundation

"The J.M. Kaplan Fund is small as foundations go, but its impact has been enormous—I think of it as Archimedes' lever, sufficient to move the world if positioned the right way. The fund has always used its resources creatively and brilliantly, with the passion, social values, and intellect of its founding family as its guide. I can think of no other philanthropy of its size that has had the impact of the Kaplan Fund, which has been at the vanguard of the preservation, environmental, and social justice movements for several generations. If it had only saved Carnegie Hall and built the Westbeth artists' housing complex, its position in the history of New York City would be significant. Roberta Gratz's history shows us that those great urban victories are but the most visible of the Kaplan Fund's many achievements."

—Paul Goldberger, architecture critic and author of
*Why Architecture Matters*

"In Roberta Gratz's exhilarating account, the stewards of the family-run Kaplan Fund emerge as modern-day Medicis. Patrons of the arts and artists, defenders of the natural and built environments. They have blocked the wreckers' ball from Carnegie Hall, Broadway Theaters, and middle-class neighborhoods, championed mass transit over super highways that would strangle urban traffic. In the course of half a century they have raised activist philanthropy to a fine art."

—John Berendt, author of *Midnight in the Garden of Good and Evil*

# IT'S A
# HELLUVA
# TOWN

**Joan K. Davidson,** *the* **J.M. Kaplan Fund,**
*and the* **Fight** *for a* **Better New York**

Roberta Brandes Gratz

**BOLD TYPE BOOKS**
New York

Bold Type Books
116 East 16th Street, 8th Floor New York, NY 10003
www.boldtypebooks.org
@BoldTypeBooks

Printed in the United States of America

First Edition: November 2020

Published by Bold Type Books, an imprint of Perseus Books, LLC, a subsidiary of Hachette Book Group, Inc. Bold Type Books is a co-publishing venture of the Type Media Center and Perseus Books.

The Hachette Speakers Bureau provides a wide range of authors for speaking events. To find out more, go to www.hachettespeakersbureau.com or call (866) 376-6591.

The publisher is not responsible for websites (or their content) that are not owned by the publisher.

Print book interior design by Trish Wilkinson.

Library of Congress Control Number: 2020942481

ISBNs: 978-1-64503-686-9 (hardcover), 978-1-64503-684-5 (e-book)

LSC-C

1 2020

# CONTENTS

# PREFACE

## *Moving Forward*

Joan K. Davidson

On a moonlit June night in 2017, more than five hundred New Yorkers gathered at the Cooper Hewitt Museum on Manhattan's Upper East Side to salute Joan K. Davidson on her ninetieth birthday and celebrate seventy years of the J.M. Kaplan Fund, of which she was president for sixteen years, from

1

1977 to 1993. The lush garden of this Georgian mansion—built for the Gilded Age tycoon Andrew Carnegie—and its elegant conservatory was a fitting site to honor a woman of great style and high civic impact. This was not meant to be five hundred of Joan's nearest and dearest friends. It was, instead, a special gathering of what she always called the "good people," those active citizens on the front lines of creative, often pathbreaking ventures that she had supported as a colleague, funder, or both.

She had joined the good people in fights to save the Hudson from the ravages of a Con Ed power plant at Storm King Mountain. She had helped create the first affordable housing for artists. She had joined and supported those who had fought against a proposed superhighway along the edge of Manhattan. She had worked to preserve the landmarks of the city without freezing progress, to create new organizations to protect and further civil liberties, and to provide legal help for communities threatened by overdevelopment. She had not won every fight: Broadway theaters had fallen despite her best efforts to protect them from the hostile, anti-urban designs of an out-of-scale hotel developer, and there were other losses as well. But overall, hers was a record of astonishing success in repairing and carrying New York forward after the madness called urban renewal.

Present that night were environmentalists, historic preservationists, urban farmers, parks restorers, civil liberties activists, authors, poets, artists, upstate activists, museum curators, community defenders, musicians, and trendsetters of every kind—what one attendee called an "only in New York" crowd.

No one gawked to see if any beautiful people might be in attendance. A number of them were indeed there, but this was not that kind of party.

Many attendees knew each other—they had joined forces on some civic initiative or had started a new organizational effort together. All had, in one way or another, worked with and admired Joan as she and her family's foundation supported—and often directly enabled—this eclectic group in their efforts to repair and transform New York City, the Hudson Valley, and other areas of New York State over more than five decades. Margot Wellington, former executive director of the Municipal

Joan K. Davidson speaks at the Cooper Hewitt celebration of seventy years of the J.M. Kaplan Fund and her ninetieth birthday.
CREDIT: THE J.M. KAPLAN FUND

Art Society (MAS), observed: "If a gas attack that night had wiped out the crowd, the city would move backward; these were all the people who moved the city forward." Joan, of course, couldn't have been more pleased with the turnout. "All those smiling faces," she noted to me with a laugh.

Manhattan borough president Gale Brewer thanked Joan on behalf of millions of unknowing New Yorkers. Kent Barwick—former head of the MAS, former chairman of the Landmarks Preservation Commission under Mayor Edward I. Koch, and longtime friend of Joan's who worked with her at the New York State Council on the Arts and on the 2008 Quadricentennial Commission—noted, "Thinking of all those good campaigns and occasional hopeless causes over many years, Joan always made it fun. . . . But when there's work to be done, when there are plots to be thickened, when there are titans to be schmoozed, it's good to know who can be counted on to bring us forward."

Peter Davidson, chairman of the J.M. Kaplan Fund, spoke for the third Kaplan generation now in charge of the Fund, noting that a fourth generation was "coming of age." He put the Fund in an interesting historical perspective: "A century ago, NYC was the center of the foundation world. Almost all were family led and focused their grant making locally. Now very few family foundations remain here in NYC and even fewer focus locally. We are proud to be family led and proud to continue to fund in our hometown and hope to remain this way for generations to come!"

The Fund was not the richest or most prominent foundation, and it was not usually a big-bucks donor.[1] However, it was often an early one, helping efforts get started and grow, mobilizing the civic energy to bring positive change, repairing past mistakes, or funding an innovative path. Everyone at the party could attest to that fact.

The Fund's concerns under Joan's leadership fell into three broad fields: historic preservation—from Gracie Mansion to humble beach cottages—protection of neighborhoods, and rescue of threatened properties; the environment, covering the protection of natural resources and conserving of open land; and culture and civil liberties, the arts, and freedom of expression—from legal support for risky things, to backing the American Civil Liberties Union (ACLU), to the publication of books. Combined, those efforts transformed New York City and beyond for more than half a century. The work of Joan and the Fund reflects the swiftly changing character of New York and reveals new insights about and understanding of the city and state's history. That is the story of this book.

# 1

# PRACTICE, PRACTICE, PRACTICE

The year was 1959. Carnegie Hall, by then standing for nearly seventy years, was scheduled for demolition. Less than ten blocks to the northwest, Lincoln Center was under construction, the brainchild of Robert Moses and John D. Rockefeller III. The New York Philharmonic had announced plans to move to Lincoln Center from Carnegie, into a venue named for the group: Philharmonic Hall.[1] Until then, the internationally acclaimed orchestra had rented Carnegie Hall, filling its stage for the bulk of the year. The orchestra could have purchased the historic home it revered, but the lure of a concert hall with its name on it was persuasive enough to make the new Lincoln Center the orchestra's permanent home. Decades later, in 2004, frustrated by the inferior acoustics of Philharmonic Hall, the orchestra announced it was moving back to Carnegie. For unknown reasons, that never happened.

Carnegie, with its unrivaled acoustics, has long been considered one of the most prestigious performance venues in the world for both classical and popular music. The soft brown

Vol. 43, No. 11 · September 9, 1957

# A RED TOWER REPLACING CARNEGIE HALL

The building boom that has been making over the old brownstone face of Manhattan with new façades of gleaming aluminum, green glass and copper-tinted steel will reach a new degree of flamboyance in the skyscraper to be erected on the site of Carnegie Hall. When the famous concert place is demolished in 1959, a new office building faced in panels of bright red porcelain will go up in its place. To liven up the effect even more, Architects Pomerance and Breines have offset the building's windows in diagonal instead of vertical rows to produce a strange-looking checkerboard pattern. Standing on stilts sunk in a broad plaza, the $22 million building will rise 44 floors above 57th Street.

All this was saddening news to the music lovers who have come to cherish old Victorian Carnegie Hall. Built as a business venture by Andrew Carnegie, a lover of Scotch bagpipe music, it opened in 1891 with a program partly conducted by Tchaikovsky. It became home for the New York Philharmonic and a magnet for the great musicians of the world. When it is demolished, U.S. music will lose one of its most acoustically perfect halls. But there was some good news for music lovers. As the office building goes up, Carnegie Hall's activities will move to Manhattan's new Lincoln Square cultural center and into a modern auditorium adjoining the new Metropolitan Opera House.

CARNEGIE HALL will offer two more full seasons of concerts and recitals before building is razed.

RED SKYSCRAPER will be reached from the street level by a foot bridge spanning its sunken plaza. ➤

The office tower proposed as replacement for Carnegie Hall in 1960 was called the "Red Menace."
CREDIT: MEREDITH CORP.

masonry building with terra-cotta and brownstone details, designed by William Burnet Tuthill, was built by steel magnate and philanthropist Andrew Carnegie and sold to real estate developer Robert Simon in 1925. Simon wanted the West 57th Street hall to remain a performance venue, but in 1959, with its major tenant planning to leave for new quarters and not enough other performing companies filling the stage, Carnegie Hall did not seem to have a bright future. Lincoln Center was rapidly emerging as a rival, and competition with it would be formidable. Thus, Carnegie Hall was sold to a new developer who planned to demolish it to build a forty-story, bright-red skyscraper. World famous violinist and conductor Isaac Stern called it the "Red Menace."[2] Stern, with both the financial and political backing of Jacob M. Kaplan, best known for successfully growing the Welch's grape juice company and establishing the J.M. Kaplan Fund, led the successful battle to save Carnegie Hall. It is the earliest and perhaps most famous rescue that would not have occurred without the J.M. Kaplan Fund. Scores of other battles with great impact would follow.

The successful campaign to save Carnegie Hall—a story that will be told in this book—was an early and significant victory at a time of many struggles over the future of New York City. At this time, Robert Moses's slum clearance was in full swing. The head of twelve public agencies—including highways, slum clearance, and parks—Moses was at the height of his power, erasing, rebuilding, or undermining much of the city from end to end.[3] On the Upper West Side alone, blocks and blocks of brownstones, apartment houses, loft buildings, and small businesses were lost to the Moses bulldozer. The rescue of Carnegie Hall more than a half century ago is forgotten by many and unknown to many more. Yet, this eleventh-hour save set the stage for similarly high-impact conflicts involving historic buildings, public spaces, cultural programs, highways, and environmental challenges that unfolded over the following years. Much had been torn down. The city was hurting; repairs were called for. New innovative efforts of all kinds emerged to help renew the city's strength and add to its wealth of physical attractions and cultural appeal. These programs were funded in many different ways.

This book is about an activist philanthropy, the J.M. Kaplan Fund, that moved beyond grant giving and invested in some unknown but innovative individuals—those who had good ideas and a certain something of character but maybe only a slim track record. This activist philanthropy had leaders who trusted their instincts and offered their hands-on advice, connections, and funding. No elaborate studies or extensive paperwork were asked for, just a creative idea, even if risky, and the commitment to see it through.[4]

In so many ways, the Fund instigated, nourished, expanded, and funded efforts that repaired and transformed New York City. The Fund's impact can be found in the New School, Westbeth, the Public Theater, the Cooper Hewitt Museum, the MAS, and the American Federation of Arts. It was present in fights over the Westway and Save the Theaters. Its mark can be seen on many landmarks, like South Street Seaport and Sailors' Snug Harbor, and on the Greenmarkets and the Coalition for the Homeless. It was involved in the protection of open space from development, the creation of vest-pocket parks, advancing the historic preservation movement, and many other initiatives. Up along the Hudson Valley, there were legal battles to protect the river and stimulate the early environmental movement, preservation efforts to save built heritage, land acquisition policies to protect the New York City watershed and create roadblocks to out-of-control sprawl, and new organizations to improve multiple aspects of Hudson Valley life and culture. By the late 1950s and early '60s, the aftermath of the urban renewal demolition derby was evident all over the city. New York was hurting, but an uncounted number of people cared enough to fight the bulldozer and find creative ways to push back and move forward at the same time. Their stories are presented here. The J.M. Kaplan Fund stood up and backed their cause.

There have been many extraordinary New York City philanthropies that have been a force for positive change. Many still are. But the legacy of the J.M. Kaplan Fund is unique: a small, family-run, well-informed activist organization with a big impact. Sometimes the Fund was the first supporter of a project, sometimes just an early one, but its funding was always pivotal. The distinguishing Kaplan trademark was not just providing funding, but embracing a roll-up-the-sleeves activism that became visible over many years of activity. First it was Jacob M. Kaplan's hands-on involvement, and then that of his eldest child, Joan Davidson, who succeeded him as president. There were also activist efforts from the Fund's small staff: Raymond S. Rubinow, Suzanne Davis, Anthony "Tony" C. Wood, and Henry Ng.

Through its work, the J.M. Kaplan Fund changed New York City and, in a more modest but similarly significant way, New York State. In focusing on the story of the Fund, this book will put city and state history in perspective, recalling events and people that have been easily forgotten—a mini history of postwar New York's physical and cultural change. Collectively, these controversies and civic efforts shaped today's city and state. While there are always scores of players involved in any civic story, one foundation, the J.M. Kaplan Fund, was consistently at the center of them all. Today's New York City cannot be fully understood or appreciated without knowing these stories. Recalling what unfolded in the past provides a useful perspective for the challenges of the present.

## THE CITY THEN

It is difficult today to fully comprehend the dramatic change that New York City underwent in the mid-twentieth century. Park Avenue north of Grand Central Station was being transformed with new office towers in the International Style. Sixth Avenue would follow and be renamed the Avenue of the Americas. The public focus was on the new. All over the city, historic buildings and sites were destroyed. Urban renewal, the federal program to rebuild cities in a newly planned way, was in full swing.[5]

Robert Caro's Pulitzer Prize–winning *The Power Broker* definitively outlines the extraordinary impact Moses had on the city and state. Caro notes, "Most cities approached urban renewal with caution. But in New York City, urban renewal was directed by Robert Moses. By 1957, $133,000,000 of public monies had been expended on urban renewal in all the cities of the United States with the exception of New York; $267,000,000 had been spent in New York."[6]

At the time, intelligent people had good reason to think that NYC was doomed, and that making it more accessible to suburbia (and cars) and easier and safer as a venue for night-time entertainment (via Lincoln Center) was the way to save it. For the most part, people accepted the notion, promoted by both federal programs and Madison Avenue ads, that cities were finished and suburbs, with their automobile-enabled life-style, were the future.[7]

The bulldozer worked overtime in cities across the nation. Neighborhoods were wiped out in a modernization effort whose scale is unimaginable today. New residential towers, some for the poor and some for the middle class, were under construction seemingly everywhere. De-densification, the purposeful thinning out of the population, was not what it was called in those days, but that was the end result. The public housing and middle-income "towers in the park" never replaced the number of residential apartments that had been torn down, the blocks and blocks of tightly packed buildings that included apartment houses, row houses, stores, small manufacturing buildings, and institutions like schools. None of the manufacturers or small businesses were replaced. This pattern played out in cities nationwide. Density was lost wherever these blocks were erased. As Jane Jacobs pointed out in *The Death and Life of Great American Cities*, Stuyvesant Town—with 125 dwellings per net acre, or 25 percent ground coverage—was a lower density than compact Greenwich Village, which had almost total ground coverage.

The World War II years had seen urban needs postponed. Resources had been directed away from cities and toward the war effort. When funding was available again, it was sent to the suburbs. The federal urban renewal program, in the two decades after World War II, demolished 404,000 low- and middle-income urban units, replacing them with only 41,580 units for the same population.[8] In New York City, Caro explains, "the housing [Moses] built to replace the housing he tore down was, to an overwhelming extent, not housing for the poor, but for the rich."[9]

A significant portion of the densely built and highly centralized heart of urban America was destroyed during these years, causing huge social and economic disruptions in whole regions, which fed the decline of cities. Many of the resulting holes in the economic, social, and physical urban fabric remain.[10] Throughout this process, projects and policies feeding the decline of cities were cloaked in the guise of noble intentions.

The 1970s proved to be no better, following on the heels of the urban riots of the '60s. As Clyde Haberman writes in a 2017 *New York Times* Editorial Observer column about a movie theater's screening of a series of films from the decade:

The '70s was the decade of the serial killer Son of Sam and of a nightmarish 1977 power blackout that led to widespread looting and vandalism. They were the "Bronx is burning" years. The municipal treasury was broke. City workers—garbage collectors, hospital workers, police officers—went on strike, heedless that it made them lawbreakers. Systemic police corruption abounded: Think "Serpico." Crime soared, with 62 percent more murders (1,814 in 1980) than there had been at the decade's start (1,117 in 1970). Some Fortune 500 companies relocated to other parts of the country. Broadway theaters moved up the evening curtain by an hour so that playgoers could get out of Times Square before the muggers took over.[11]

The physical city was going through a radical transformation as well. New York neighborhoods featuring combinations of brownstones, small tenements, and modest-scale apartment houses mixed in with small businesses, small factories, schools, and churches were being replaced with high-rise buildings— residential only—surrounded by lawns enclosed by fences and signs reading "Keep off the grass." Many of the lost structures were of incomparable architectural beauty; most were just of solid construction and useful for their residential, industrial, or institutional occupant. Few people realized that the new number of residential units was less than what was being lost. "[Moses] had built more housing than any public official in history, but the city was starved for housing, more starved, if possible, than when he started building," notes Caro, to the disbelief of many.[12] Furthermore, few of the factories and storefronts were being replaced at all, as many of those businesses left the city for good. The focus was on modernity, cleaning up the neglected and run-down city, and, worst of all, separating uses.[13]

In postwar America, everything new was the coin of the realm. New suburbs, new highways, new cars, new dishwashers, new fashions, new cities. Nowhere was this urban vision more evident than on the Upper West Side of Manhattan, where the biggest and most pathbreaking of all urban renewal projects was constructed: Lincoln Center.[14]

Planned since the 1950s under the leadership of John D. Rockefeller III and Robert Moses, the self-contained Lincoln Center was underway, slowly but surely, overseen by the Committee on Slum Clearance of the City of New York, of which Moses was the head. Rockefeller's leadership position in the city's business and arts community guaranteed critical public

Lincoln Center in 1969, shortly after completion
CREDIT: CHARLES ROTKIN / GETTY IMAGES

support.[15] As the *New York Times* notes in a piece marking the fiftieth season of the Metropolitan Opera, "There was the sheer scope of the artistic megaproject that was the Met and Lincoln Center, muscled through by mid-20th-century power brokers, including Robert Moses and John D. Rockefeller III, who wanted an American cultural acropolis."[16] Rockefeller was made the inaugural president of Lincoln Center in 1956 and became its chairman in 1961.

The 16.3-acre complex is the first known cultural mall of its kind in the country. It brought together—in one street-less place, imposed on and separate from the urban grid—a mix of arts and educational institutions: music, ballet, opera, theater, a library, a law school, and a performing arts school. It had a national impact, changing the way cities developed or redeveloped their cultural institutions. Other metropolises would follow the pattern, creating a one-stop cultural island, a separate enclave for assorted arts institutions. Previously, these institutions had been located on their own sites in different areas—becoming neighborhood anchors, as Carnegie Hall was—but this old pattern was considered an anachronism. Better that these institutions be developed in close proximity to each other and be easily accessible to car-driving visitors, the new thinking went.

It is difficult to be critical of Lincoln Center's physical form without people assuming the criticism is also directed at the cultural content. The content—the theater, opera, ballet, concerts, and outdoor life—is of the highest quality and deservedly loved and admired.[17] But form and content are two very different things, too often confused as being one and the same.

Lincoln Center embodied a misguided formula for reviving struggling downtowns across America and seeking new ways to compete with the suburbs. Automobile friendly and effectively cut off from the supposedly dangerous city, Lincoln Center was meant to appeal to fearful suburbanites and local residents. This was early in the trend of cities trying to compete with the suburbs by becoming car centric. Individually, the separate buildings were the epitome of the new architectural trend of modernism. In the immediate years after Lincoln Center opened, people went there and then drove directly home, having no positive impact on the surrounding neighborhood.

In the late 1960s and '70s, the West Side began its own organic regeneration, as urban pioneers restored blighted brownstones, and restaurants and new stores opened in the area further north. Only after the neighborhood began its comeback did Lincoln Center–goers venture beyond its borders. Mistakenly, Lincoln Center is credited with the turnaround of the Upper West Side, but since that change was happening in other historic, decidedly urban neighborhoods in New York— and in cities around the country—it is difficult to attribute the slow rebirth to Lincoln Center.[18]

The social and financial impact of the serial relocation of families from one urban renewal site to another can never be measured statistically, but it is something that should always be kept in mind when focusing on this era, or even more recent periods of massive displacement.[19] Few remember, if they were ever aware, that Lincoln Center displaced 1,647 families and 383 businesses in 188 buildings.[20] The human cost of this widespread clearance is rarely recognized. Elizabeth Yeampierre, a

Thousands of San Juan Hill's residential and commercial buildings were destroyed to make way for Lincoln Center.
CREDIT: EDDIE HAUSNER / THE *NEW YORK TIMES* / REDUX

Brooklyn lawyer and citywide leader of the city's environmental justice movement, recalls:

> My family lived on the Upper West Side, in a blue-collar community. We had a family infrastructure that made it possible for the women in my family to work, for the children to be cared for, and although we were not wealthy by any means, we were doing okay. When we were displaced, we became "roadkill" in Robert Moses' vision. Our family was scattered to the Bronx to Queens and throughout Manhattan. I went to five schools in eight years, and, in my family, some people went on to be drug addicts and some women went on public

19

assistance. The entire fabric of my family was destroyed as a result of that displacement.[21]

Several areas of this Upper West Side neighborhood were leveled. Considered blighted and ostensibly at the end of their useful life, many of the elegant brownstones and small apartment houses that were demolished were no different from the buildings commanding extraordinary sums today, whether on the Upper West Side or in other neighborhoods all over the city. Many survivors have been lovingly restored more than

The demolition of blocks of West Side buildings to make way for Lincoln Center was postponed for the filming of *West Side Story*.
CREDIT: ROLLS PRESS / GETTY IMAGES

once since those years when they were considered beyond redemption. The past recedes from memory all too quickly. We are accustomed to accepting change in the name of progress without taking a questioning look backward. Worship of the new preempted everything during these pivotal postwar decades.

## PROGRESSIVE PROJECTS
## RENEW THE CITY

Thus, it is necessary to recognize the degree of urban destruction unfolding in New York after World War II to fully appreciate the energy and devotion demonstrated by a wide array of tenacious civic activists. The J.M. Kaplan Fund's support was clear in many of these rescue efforts, not just the groups fighting against neighborhood clearance. The Fund supported grassroots groups working to rebuild and address the poverty and wretched housing conditions at the root of so much urban decay, such as the Cooper Square Committee, led by the indomitable Frances Goldin, which organized to stop a Robert Moses clearance plan and instead established a mutual housing association with twenty-two buildings that stabilized its East Village neighborhood.

J.M. Kaplan's experience growing up in slums of Chelsea, Massachusetts, (see Chapter 2) clearly influenced his belief in decent, affordable housing and public parks as human rights. In the late 1950s, he heard a young social worker offer new ideas about addressing youthful crime and poverty on the Lower East Side at a benefit dinner of the Henry Street Settlement, where J.M.'s wife, Alice, served on the board. He liked what he heard and suggested a program, overseen by the Henry Street Settlement, that evolved into the much-admired Mobilization for Youth (MFY). MFY gained the support of many foundations and became the model for a substantial national, federally subsidized anti-poverty program aimed at youth.

These were the early days of community-led anti-poverty efforts. Social justice issues were all over the J.M. Kaplan Fund's grant making, including support for United Neighborhood Houses, Grand Street Settlement, Hudson Guild Neighborhood House, Freedom House, and Citizens Housing and Planning Council (led by Ira Robbins, a personal friend of Kaplan's). "The '60s saw a proliferation of youth gangs and a growing awareness of poverty," recalled architect and planner Ron Shiffman, an early leader in these efforts as founding director of the Pratt Center for Community Development, in an interview. "This, coupled with the emerging civil rights movement, led a select number of foundations to fund innovative approaches to addressing urban, racial and community development issues. Ford, Kaplan, Rockefeller Brothers Fund, Astor were leaders in that effort," Shiffman added.

Over the years, a handful of individuals shaped and administered the Fund's aims and grants, including Joan Davidson. In the early 1960s, Joan was living in Oregon and then Alaska and raising four children. She was involved in national Democratic Party politics with her husband, C. Girard Davidson. A native of Lafayette, Louisiana, Davidson was a lawyer and former undersecretary of the interior from 1946 to 1950 in the Harry S. Truman and Lyndon B. Johnson administrations.

He had been the divorced father of one of Joan's third-grade pupils when she was a teacher at the Georgetown Day School.

Joan had long exhibited the same deep interest in the arts that her mother, Alice, had displayed. In the early '60s, from afar and with periodic NYC visits, Joan was already involved in Fund work. By 1967, she was separated from her husband and ready to return from the Northwest to New York permanently. J.M. appointed her vice president of the Fund and she dug in.

Before Joan came on board in a big way, the Fund's chief staff member and activist about town was handsome, elegant Ray Rubinow. Hired by J.M. in 1955, Rubinow was a born troubleshooter and happy lieutenant for J.M.'s causes. Rubinow was born in Palestine to social-justice-minded parents; his father was a doctor working on behalf of the poor. The family left when Rubinow was young, and he led a peripatetic life through college. In the 1930s, he described himself by the then-new term "philanthropoid," working for the Julius Rosenwald Fund in Chicago, a pathbreaking socially concerned foundation endowed by the part owner and leader of Sears, Roebuck and Company. In Chicago, Rubinow was also a leader of the League for Industrial Democracy.

From there, he moved to New York and got involved in Reform Democratic politics and met J.M. Kaplan. "JM was both an FDR fan and critic and also an admirer of Governor Herbert Lehman. He wrote letters to his favorite Supreme Court justices about injustices as he saw them," said Joan. Rubinow's and J.M.'s interests meshed perfectly, and J.M.'s vast political connections were always helpful in Rubinow's activities. As a team, they were strategic and politically skillful.

Tony Wood—whose book *Preserving New York: Winning the Right to Protect a City's Landmarks* is the definitive history of the New York City Landmarks Law—worked at the J.M. Kaplan Fund from 1986 to 1993. He said of Rubinow, "J.M. was a wily strategist. He hired and invested in Ray, who served as both his 'research and development department' and 'SWAT team activist.' He let him loose where necessary."

Joan added, "Ray went to all the community board meetings and was famous for frequently raising his hand, crying, 'Query, query!' He knew everything that was going on."

Kent Barwick noted in conversation that Rubinow was a similar attention-getter at huge Fund meetings. "It was an old union-hall trick," Barwick said with a laugh. "He would stand in the back and call, 'Query,' getting everyone's attention."

Suzanne Davis was hired to be Rubinow's assistant and noted that he was often "out saving the world"—as we will see later in Chapter 7, regarding the Fund's involvement in the early environmental movement. While he was out of the office, Davis recalled, "he left me to run the foundation and taught me to become a philanthropoid too, because I—who started as his assistant and knew *nothing* about the nonprofit world— gradually took over the administration." Rubinow was a great admirer of Rachel Carson and Jane Jacobs and an inveterate writer of letters of advice to US presidents. "I never saw any responses," Davis added.

The landmarks preservation movement in New York didn't fully evolve until the 1970s, but the Fund's efforts certainly helped plant the seeds for its eventual success. While the Carnegie Hall fight was focused more on culture than architecture, the Fund succeeded in preserving both. That rescue effort actually started with a connection to the New School. In the mid-1950s, J.M. began his decades of generous support for the university, long considered an important center of New York City intellectual life. Founded during World War I by a group of European refugees, the New School for Social Research, as it was first known, struggled financially for decades. J.M. began supporting it in 1957, modestly at first but with increasing commitment. For a long time, he served as chairman of the university's board. The New School grew in intellectual,

J.M. Kaplan talking to Alvin Johnson, longtime president of the New School, and Albert A. List (L).
CREDIT: NEW SCHOOL PHOTOGRAPH COLLECTION, NS.04.01.01, BOX 14, FOLDER 1, NEW SCHOOL ARCHIVES AND SPECIAL COLLECTIONS, THE NEW SCHOOL, NEW YORK, NEW YORK

educational, and political importance but always seemed to struggle financially. Eventually, J.M. and another board member, New York philanthropist Albert A. List, became the primary funders. Together, they put the school on solid financial footing and led a fundraising campaign that added two buildings, both of which are named after Kaplan and List.

Primarily because of Alice Kaplan's deep love of classical music, the Fund supported many music programs at the New School over the years, including the university's affordable chamber music concert series and the young audiences series in the city's public schools.[22] Violinist Alexander Schneider was the founding artistic director of the concert program, and he and the Kaplans became fast friends. Celebrated violinist Isaac Stern and Schneider were already longtime friends. Schneider introduced Stern to the Kaplans, and they also "instantly became friends," Stern recalled in an interview.[23]

## SAVING CARNEGIE HALL

In 1959, after numerous public demonstrations protesting the planned demise of Carnegie Hall and a grassroots rescue effort, Stern decided to get in front and lead the cause. Isaac and Vera Stern immediately called on Alice and J.M. Kaplan. When Stern explained the issue, J.M. got closely involved. His immediate acceptance of the idea "is what made it possible to form the committee," Stern told me. J.M. gave the first $25,000 to hire a coordinator, and he assigned Rubinow to act on his behalf. In January 1960, the Committee to Save Carnegie Hall was formed.

"Do you think my father cared about classical music?" Joan asked in an interview with me.

He probably had never set foot in Carnegie Hall. But he responded to Isaac. He got excited. He said absolutely I'm going to help you and he put Ray full-time on the Carnegie fight. He, my aging father himself, spent his days going up to Albany to lobby the Legislature and down to D.C. to lobby Senators. And I'm afraid he hasn't gotten much acknowledgement for this, only a tiny nameplate in the Carnegie upstairs hall. That's the way he was. Once he got exercised about an idea, in part because the right person had presented it, he went all out.[24]

This was no easy battle. "It seemed almost insurmountable," Stern said, as soon as we began our conversation in his spacious apartment on Central Park West. "The Rockefellers were building Lincoln Center. The whole power structure was behind them—the business and financial communities, cultural leaders, politicians, and urban renewal officials. I went to the Rockefeller Foundation to suggest they include the purchase of Carnegie Hall as part of Lincoln Center. It could have been bought for a couple million dollars. I met with a young man named Dean Rusk [the president of the Rockefeller Foundation].[25] He took it seriously and took it to his board. After considering it, they said no, they weren't interested; they were building Lincoln Center."

J.M. opened political doors for the rescue effort. Stern wrote letters to all the great musicians of the world. State legislation was proposed and passed by June 1960, enabling the city to buy Carnegie Hall and issue bonds to pay for it. "Governor [Nelson] Rockefeller wrote the most beautiful support letter for the legislation, despite the fact that his brother [John] was building Lincoln Center," Stern noted with a sense of irony. "He recognized the validity of the reason for Carnegie Hall's continuation."

But most of the activity to secure bipartisan support was kept out of public view. "We quietly lobbied, I personally lobbied, each member of the city council," Stern said. "The one who really helped was Mayor [Robert F.] Wagner." In the spring, Stern and Wagner attended an ecumenical Passover seder, held on Central Park West, near Stern's home. They left together. "I invited him up for a cold beer afterward," Stern recalled, "saying I had something I wanted to talk about." Wagner responded to Stern's pitch immediately, telling him that he was "an honorary member of the musicians' union and that he had gone to the children's concerts with Damrosch.[26] [Wagner] guided us, opened doors. . . . His help was incalculable. We went with our hat in hand to the council and lobbied each of the members. The establishment didn't want it. There was an enormous real estate investment [at stake] here." Nevertheless, the city legislation approved the designation of Carnegie Hall as a national historic landmark, a federal category, and stipulated the property could not be sold to a private developer. "There was a lot of pressure back and forth," Stern said.

At some point, a meeting with the mayor was suggested in order to talk about financial matters, and "I said I would be glad to have that kind of meeting with two provisos: that I come to represent Carnegie Hall and Rockefeller come to represent Lincoln Center and that we have a press conference afterward," Stern explained. "The meeting never took place. . . . The newspapers were on our side." After considering it, Rockefeller had "backed out. I wanted to debate Rockefeller in public. No way could we match the enormous political and financial power. They didn't want the death of Carnegie Hall on their backs" or to be known as "those who killed Carnegie Hall."

There is no doubt, as Stern said, that this effort had "seemed insurmountable," which is why J.M.'s involvement was so crucial. Stern said emphatically, "Without Jack Kaplan's complete and utter devotion and money to back it, we couldn't have organized [the bipartisan effort] to the extent that we did. . . . J.M. was all about keeping the artistic viability of the city for artists."

In addition to challenging politicians and financiers, the struggle to save Carnegie Hall engaged members of New York's philanthropic community. Brooke Astor, who in 1960 had become president of the Vincent Astor Foundation, was impressed by the tenacious leadership of Kaplan and Stern. Linda Gillies, longtime director of the Vincent Astor Foundation, recalled for me that "Mrs. Astor, who was passionate about preservation, often said that the successful Carnegie Hall effort taught her how philanthropy could play a key role in saving New York City's precious historic resources." Preservation became a priority for the foundation, Gillies adds, which over subsequent decades often collaborated with the J.M. Kaplan Fund.

Stern was the first president of Carnegie Hall and remained in that role until his death in 2001. For years, the hall ran financially close to the bone. Eventually, a new deal was struck for the city to buy the building for $5 million in 1960 and transfer it to the Carnegie Hall Corporation. In 1986, some of the biggest names in New York City philanthropy led a comprehensive restoration and expansion effort, including Brooke Astor, Sanford Weill, James Wolfensohn, Felix Rohatyn, and Elihu Rose. Carnegie Hall remains, to this day, the premier concert venue.

As Stern noted, "Carnegie Hall is not a building. It is a reflection of America. Every important musician, conductor and orchestra has performed there. That's where you came to be judged as significant. It is synonymous with America's place in the sun. It was then and is now synonymous with this country. . . . We were lucky that Philharmonic Hall came out so badly. It worked in our favor enormously. . . . Lincoln Center is enormous and has a lot there . . . but we had acoustics and history and you don't earn that overnight."

## MORE THREATENED HERITAGE

Carnegie Hall was saved but, as noted, the '60s was a period of unimaginable urban destruction. The 1910 beaux arts Pennsylvania Station—the majestic McKim, Mead & White masterpiece with the waiting room modeled after the Baths of Caracalla in Rome—saw its multiyear demolition begin in 1963, before the 1965 Landmarks Law. The save Penn Station effort was a failure that the Fund supported. A small committee picketed in front of the building, led by a group of caring architects, activists, and writers, including Rubinow and

Richard Kaplan, J.M.'s son. Rubinow served on the committee and brought Kaplan resources with him, but to no avail. Architect Peter Samton remembered, "Ray brought the nonarchitects, like Jane Jacobs and [arts writer] Aline Saarinen" to the cause. "He also brought J.M.'s financial support."

Even the newspapers editorialized about the plundering of the city's heritage; something rarely seen since. Ada Louise Huxtable famously wrote in the *New York Times*, "Any city gets what it admires, will pay for, and ultimately, deserves. Even when we had Penn Station, we couldn't afford to keep it clean. We want and deserve tin-can architecture in a tin-horn culture. And we will probably be judged not by the monuments we build but by those we have destroyed."[27]

While the Landmarks Law was being considered in the city council, the elaborate French Renaissance Brokaw Mansion at 79th Street and Fifth Avenue went down. The 1883 Metropolitan Opera House at 39th and Broadway was demolished in 1967, after the Landmarks Preservation Commission declined to designate it. The 1908 Singer Building, the first skyscraper in the Financial District, also went down in 1967. And, of course, whole neighborhoods—with the architectural, cultural, and social touchstones of so many lives—fell under the bulldozer.

The principal mover behind the city's dramatic physical change, as noted, was master builder Robert Moses, who was probably the city's most polarizing figure. He is most favorably known for his 1920s creation of Jones Beach on the south shore of Long Island, but even it had highway overpasses too low for public buses to take carless people to the beach.[28] Moses also built new parks and dramatically altered many existing ones around the city. But, as Robert Caro notes, "he built parks and playgrounds with a lavish hand, but they were parks and playgrounds for the rich and the comfortable. Recreational facilities for the poor he doled out like a miser."[29]

## THE LOWER MANHATTAN EXPRESSWAY

New Yorkers were also gearing up for a fight against Moses's plan to put a road through Washington Square Park. For decades, Greenwich Village residents had tried unsuccessfully to stem the loss of historic buildings on the north and south sides of the park. Their activism was broad-based and successful only in staving off what increasingly seemed like the inevitable. Over time, all the historic buildings on the south side went down to make way for structures owned by New York University (NYU) and the Catholic Church.[30] The one exception is the 1890 Judson Memorial Church, designed by Stanford White with stained glass by John La Farge and sculpture by Augustus Saint-Gaudens. On the north side, at Fifth Avenue, a white-brick apartment house replaced the incomparable 1840s Rhinelander houses and two red-brick and marble mansions with wrought-iron balconies designed by Richard Upjohn, architect of Trinity Church.

Tony Wood writes: "For the entire decade of the 1950s, Washington Square Park was a civic battleground. . . . The epic struggle would help create an energy and civic momentum that would contribute to the climate of activism essential to advancing the cause of preserving the Village."[31] This added to the broader momentum demanding a law to protect historic buildings.

Starting in the 1930s, several earlier Washington Square Park redesign plans had been spearheaded by Moses, but they had been either defeated, stalled, or modified by Greenwich Village activists. One Moses plan would have cut off the corners of the park and eliminated the fountain. But he fought hardest and longest for a road through the park—a plan revived in 1952—that would have eventually turned into an off-ramp for his planned Lower Manhattan Expressway. The new road would be named Fifth Avenue South, of great value to the developers who had secured the twelve square blocks south of the park, which had been cleared by Moses under urban renewal. The fight over the road through the park was bitter, a mere prelude to the battle over the expressway to come in the 1960s. (The expressway would have connected the Holland Tunnel to the Williamsburg Bridge. The two projects were linked, but Village residents didn't know that at the time of the park fight.)

Two mothers—Shirley Hayes and Edith Lyons—sitting in the park playground with their kids, recognized how destructive the road plan was and determined to fight it. Over the course of several years and at different stages of the political approval process, they circulated petitions to stop the road development that gathered four thousand, ten thousand, and, one time, thirty-five thousand signatures (without social media). But the plan was advancing anyway and would soon reach the final stop at the Board of Estimate.

Enter Ray Rubinow, fresh from the successful Carnegie Hall rescue. With Hayes and Lyons's blessing, he renamed their group the Joint Emergency Committee to Close Washington Square Park to Traffic, with a star-studded membership that included Eleanor Roosevelt, Jane Jacobs, Lewis Mumford, Norman Vincent Peale, Margaret Mead, and William H. Whyte, a friend of Jacobs's whose book *Organization Man* had become a best seller.[32] As Wood described it to me in an interview, "The civic equivalent of the marines had landed."

Jacobs, a savvy strategist, collaborated with lawyer Norman Redlich to develop a political offense that worked. This is, in effect, why Jacobs has often been identified as the leader against Moses in this effort. She was very publicly visible but was always quick to give the real credit to Hayes and Lyons, as did Moses. At a public hearing in the 1950s about the road, at which both Jacobs and Moses were in attendance, Jacobs told me in conversation, Moses stomped out after, declaring, "There is nobody against this. Nobody. Nobody. Nobody but a bunch of mothers."[33]

The committee was very crafty, asking for the park's closure to traffic on a trial basis to see what would happen. "We knew it was perfectly safe to just ask for a trial basis," Jacobs told me in an interview.[34] "We knew that if the test were successful, it would become permanent. This was nothing radical really, just a chance to experiment a little. . . . They told us: 'You will be back on your knees begging us to put the roadway back because of the inundation of traffic elsewhere.' We didn't believe that for a minute. We just said: 'We'll try it. This is an experiment.'" Traffic actually declined.[35]

The winning strategy reflected two ideas Jacobs often repeated as advice: always make sure that everything is done in the name of the larger group—in this case, the committee—and try to start with a "temporary experiment" that inevitably turns permanent. As Wood notes in his book, "After past disappointing compromises and a series of losses, the Village had finally won big."

At a packed neighborhood meeting in 1958, notable housing advocate, author, and well-known Columbia professor Charles Abrams observed, "Rebellion is brewing in America. The American city is the battleground for the preservation of [economic and cultural] diversity and Greenwich Village should be its Bunker Hill."

The Village battles, as well as equally energetic fights against Moses in Brooklyn Heights, fueled the preservation movement.[36] But there were other singular preservation successes that Rubinow and J.M. achieved. One of the city's, if not the country's, unique historic sites, the 1833 Sailors' Snug Harbor on Staten Island, was scheduled to be demolished in the early 1960s and redeveloped into high-rise structures. J.M. stepped in to help save it, not only funding most of the rescue effort but using his political connections to get the attention of elected officials. Originally the first home for retired merchant seamen, the eighty-three-acre complex has the remains of an extraordinary variety of historic architecture, including a rare row of five Greek temple–like buildings. Sailors' Snug Harbor became one of the first designations by the new Landmarks Preservation Commission, formed in 1965. Its designation prompted an early challenge to the commission's legal powers and was upheld. After its rescue, the site, considered one of New York's crown jewels, was sold to the city and is currently a cultural and botanical institution.

## SOUTH STREET SEAPORT

Even more significant for the city's evolving preservation movement was the rescue of the South Street Seaport, a twelve-square-block site where New York evolved as a port city—a symbol of its critical role in the development of the country. The site features some of the oldest architecture in downtown Manhattan, including the largest concentration in the city of restored early nineteenth-century commercial buildings. In the mid-1960s, this, too, was scheduled for demolition, until Peter and Norma Stanford organized the effort to save it. Peter Stanford had been a student at Lincoln High School with Joan. Over a drink at the old Plaza Hotel's Oak Bar, he shared with her the plight of this extraordinary remnant of nineteenth-century maritime activity, as well as his unhappiness in his ad agency job. She and J.M. provided a grant for Stanford to undertake the Seaport project and kiss his job goodbye. Joan had immediately understood the significance and brought the challenge to J.M. He shared her enthusiasm, and the South Street Seaport was launched.

Kent Barwick, then also a young advertising executive, was a volunteer at the Seaport and got to know Joan. In 1969, he became the head of the Municipal Art Society, the venerable civic organization focused on the city's built environment, in part at the suggestion and urging of Joan and others. Barwick has remained committed to the South Street Seaport Museum through all of its subsequent ups and downs. "The preservation movement as a larger movement evolved out of the major battles of the '60s, and the Seaport was the major battle of that time," he told me in an interview. "Its political success brought together many individuals with architectural interests, and many of those involved became preservation activists. It was the first coming together of people who became preservation leaders and encouraged future battles." Joan, as would be true in so many of her involvements from then on, was a critical funder, board member, and energetic participant. "There was a coherent connection among all those issues at that time," Barwick added.

While the 1960s witnessed heavy demolition all over the city, the early preservationists focused primarily on Manhattan. An early committee of the MAS, working with the historic buildings committee of the local chapter of the American Institute of Architects (AIA), was quietly putting together a list of the most important buildings to be saved, and also working behind the scenes to persuade the administration of Mayor Robert Wagner to establish a landmarks preservation law.[37]

## THE LANDMARKS LAW

Citywide civic organizations like the MAS and AIA local chapter continued to lobby vigorously to get City Planning Commission chair James Felt to deliver on his promise to address the issue of preservation once he had gotten his new zoning ordinance through the city council. Felt told them he was lobbying the mayor. At the same time, highly visible public discontent with Moses's clearance projects in several areas was having an effect on the mayor. There were the West Side defenders of the playground in Central Park (including mothers with baby carriages blocking the bulldozer), the revelations of widespread slum-clearance abuses and scandal on the Upper West Side revealed in the *New York Post*, and the highway fighters and park defenders in Greenwich Village and Brooklyn Heights.

These events all prompted Mayor Wagner to do what he often did when confronted with a sizzling hot issue: appoint a committee. The committee formed in 1961 to study a possible law, and out of that came the Landmarks Law that eventually passed, in very weak form, in 1965.[38] That first iteration only functioned for six months every three years and did not cover interiors, landscapes, or city-owned buildings. The commission wrote reports on the landmark qualification of city-owned property, but those reports were not made public, and if the commission designated a city-owned property it was not enforced.[39] All that changed in 1973, when the city council, led by Councilman Carter Burden and aided significantly by the MAS under Kent Barwick's leadership, amended and strengthened the law. The law was made to function full-time and to cover landscapes, interiors, and city-owned properties.[40]

The myth prevails that the loss of Penn Station led to the 1965 Landmarks Law. It did help fuel the long-growing public demand for legal protection for landmarks, but it was only the most egregious loss in a long line of losses. The real activity, the grassroots energy, actually came from dedicated

Demonstrators picket the planned demolition of Penn Station (L to R: Ray Rubinow of the J.M. Kaplan Fund, author Jane Jacobs, art critic Aline Saarinen, and architect Philip Johnson).
CREDIT: WALTER DARAN / GETTY IMAGES

activists. Rubinow could be counted on to lend both his time and access to J.M. Kaplan Fund money. Once the Landmarks Law was passed and the Landmarks Preservation Commission was established, it remained to the ever-expanding grassroots preservation groups around the city to be the vigilant protectors of the built environment, especially at times when the weakness of the commission was most apparent.

# 2

# THE FOUNDER

Jacob Merrill Kaplan was born in 1891, the son of poor Jewish immigrants, Felice "Fanny" Gertz Kaplan and David Chaim Levin, from Bialystok in Russian-controlled Poland. His rabbi father had come first—settling on a farm in Chelsea, Massachusetts, a rough waterfront city north of Boston—and eventually saved enough to bring his wife over from Bialystok. Jack Kaplan was born on that farm. (Fanny's first husband had died, thus her last name, Kaplan. She had one son, Abe Kaplan, who became a father figure for Jack after David Chaim Levin died when Jack was eleven. In his late teen years, Jack changed his last name and added a middle name, Merrill, because he considered it a mark of distinction.)

J.M. summed up his early life in a 1956 speech: "We were always poor. I worked from the earliest moment I can remember."[1] He started selling fruit and vegetables, and then began working as a newsboy at the age of six. He developed a number of routes, hired his friends, and left school in the eighth grade after his parents died. As he reported, he then "assumed responsibility for a family of four."

His challenging existence was made worse by the local tough boys, who picked on him for being Jewish. Joan Davidson remembered him saying many times that "he was chased after school and beaten up every day by Marky Donnelly." With an admiring tone, Joan described her father as "this tough little Jewish kid with a youth of struggle, who later remained torn between his early hardscrabble history and his later capitalist associates. He loved hanging out with the bankers, but on the other hand, he sometimes wanted to shove it to them as well." In 1956, J.M. Kaplan wrote a rather sentimental letter to his children, essentially admitting to his failings as a mostly absent father. He says of himself, "I've been a scrapper all my days. I had to fight my way out of a hard and joyless childhood. I had to fight my way through the competitive world of business. I had to fight against my own inadequacies—my lack of formal education, my tendency to feel bitter about the things I missed as a child, my desire to build success upon success."

J.M. spent years as a peddler and odd-job worker, somehow taking care of his four siblings, until he joined his older brother, first in the sugar business and then in molasses trading in the Caribbean, helping develop the business and accumulating his first fortune. The brothers moved blackstrap molasses from West Indies sugar mills—where it was considered a waste product—to untapped markets in the United States. In the 1920s, J.M. lived and worked mostly in Cuba, and he sold the company just before the 1929 crash. "Ultimately I had responsibility for managing companies that handled more than half the molasses produced in the world," he noted in that 1956 speech. In 1933, he visited the Chautauqua-Erie grape belt in upstate New York, where he had heard there was "an opportunity to buy a small grape processing plant" owned by a group of six small grape-grower cooperatives. He was appalled at the condition of the vineyards and the badly run processing plant, so he bought the plant and set about reviving the abandoned and decaying vineyards, which increased production, improved quality, and restored vigor and hope among the farmers.

Six years later, the members of the small revived cooperative joined with other growers to form a larger, stronger one. Then, in 1945, Kaplan acquired the Welch's grape juice company merged it with the processing plant, and arranged in 1956 for the cooperative to take over both the plant and Welch's, in "the largest cooperative transfer in the history of the country."[2] As Joan explained, J.M. continued to support farmers in many ways over the years, especially by buying up and preserving farmland around New York State to keep the economy secure and strong.

Welch's is the most well-known story, but J.M. Kaplan pursued many other investment ventures as well. He loved buying up real estate, especially cheap land, wherever he went. Grandson Matt Davidson was J.M.'s mentee and worked with him from 1982 until 1987, when J.M. died. Matt explained, "When we were living in Portland, my grandparents twice a year dutifully came across the country to visit the grandchildren. But after a few hours, JM had had enough of visiting, so he would find a realtor and go on the prowl for something to buy. He was very astute and he said, 'Never sell real estate, real estate sells itself.' He bought up industrial land along the Willamette River in Oregon in the 1950s for about $3,000 an

J.M. Kaplan

acre and made a killing when he sold it in the '80s. Finding the land was the fun for him; the joy of discovery. He bought land in the citrus-belt lowland in Florida and eventually gave it to the Nature Conservancy. When Oregon was building dams for hydropower, JM bought lots of industrial land before the plants arrived. His thrill was seeing something no one else could see."

Mary Kaplan, J.M.'s youngest child, added, "He had an eye for opportunity." J.M. bought land in East Hampton, Long Island, where the family had started spending summers. "He was not about to sit on the beach," Matt said, "so he bought land that could be secured in perpetuity for agriculture—and he got to gaze out over the fields."

In some ventures, Matt explained, J.M. tangled with old-line bankers "who balked at doing business with 'this fellow from New York,' so they would make a deal" very favorable to him to get rid of him. J.M.'s business interests were varied. "I remember driving with him through Georgia one time," Matt said, "and we pulled over at a little grocery, where he scanned all the shelves, searching for Welch's grape juice. Wherever he went, he pinched apples and knocked on melons. And for a while, he owned the A&P store chain." In the 1920s, A&P was the biggest retailer in the world, with its high-volume, low-price philosophy.

In 1945, Jack founded the J.M. Kaplan Fund. "Jack Kaplan had always responded instinctively and generously to human need, worked resourcefully to improve existing American institutions and to help create needed new ones, and been a port in the storm for social reformers and visionaries of many stripes unable to find encouragement elsewhere," writes Joan in the 1978 annual report of the Fund, adding that "his ideals and values had informed the work of the fund and would continue to do so." That was Joan's first full year at the helm of the Fund and the first year of annual reports, of which Joan is rightly proud. In an interview, Joan added: "He had scant idea of the Fund as an institution, with\its own character, and its own mission. He felt the Fund was mainly to be used for what he wanted it to be used for. He responded to people he liked and admired, period."[3]

Joan—tall, slim, and always elegant—is as amiable as she is smart and perceptive. Extremely gracious, she never aggressively pushes her own point of view, and even maintains that poise while arguing with people with whom she disagrees. But she does know how to get what she wants. With fashionably short white hair and a throaty laugh, she has a way with people. Joan often became friends with the leaders of the projects and programs she funded and, as an attractive divorcée when she returned to New York in the late 1960s, she was frequently linked to some of the most desirable bachelors in town.

Joan speaks of her father with enormous respect and affection. She likes to remind people of how J.M., with his white hair, bow tie, and cane, was famous for his daily walk. "The office was on 12th Street [later 34th Street] and Fifth Avenue," she told me, "and he walked home every day, from 12th Street to 80th, picking up trash as he went along. And clever people learned that when you walk along with Jack and you introduce an interesting topic you're involved with, later, very likely, a grant would emerge! Who knows how many grants went to the savvy folks who intercepted and chatted with him along those walks?" He was a "soft-touch," if you caught him at the right moment, Matt added.

In 1925, J.M. Kaplan had married Budapest-born Alice Manheim, after they met in Havana. The daughter of an upper-middle-class Jewish family, Alice was described by Matt as "Jewish nobility, graceful, artistic, educated with great

Alice Kaplan
CREDIT: THE J.M. KAPLAN FUND

taste—everything [JM] wasn't." Her strong interest in the arts influenced her children—Joan, Betty, Richard, and Mary—and the Fund's giving. She dropped out of college to marry Kaplan, but in her sixties she went to Columbia University to earn a master's degree in art history.

With a well-known "good eye," Alice amassed a notable art collection and served as president of the American Federation of Arts from 1967 to 1977, where she developed many traveling exhibitions and produced an educational film, *The Art of Seeing.*[4] She led the celebration of the fiftieth anniversary of the historic 1913 Armory Show, helped start the American Folk Art Museum, and served on museum boards (Whitney Museum of American Art) and museum committees (MoMA, Metropolitan Museum of Art). When she learned of the imminent dispersal of the Hewitt sisters' famous collection of decorative-arts material that had been on display at Cooper Union, she mobilized like-minded friends to help rescue this collection, and with it establish what has become the Cooper Hewitt, Smithsonian Design Museum. In 1982 she received the Mayor's Award for Arts and Culture.

In 2013, Joan, as president of the Furthermore book-publishing grant program, established the Alice Award to honor her mother. A press release notes, "Alice loved and collected the illustrated book as a work of art in itself and an essential document of a civilized society. The award is given annually to an illustrated book that makes a valuable contribution to its field and demonstrates high standards of production. Fields considered include the fine arts and the natural and built environments and related public issues."

Joan was born in 1927, not long before the stock market crash of 1929. She grew up during the New Deal and, when young, sat on a child-welfare committee in New York City with "a very aged" Eleanor Roosevelt. She was in college when Franklin Delano Roosevelt died, and she and her parents wept together on the telephone. She has been an ardent liberal all her life. She explained that it was mostly her values that informed the Fund's mission: "For the individual against the mass, freedom of speech, protecting the environment and historic preservation, community protection and betterment, and the arts, mainly music and the visual and literary arts." That vision was expressed in every Fund annual report.

# 3

## SOUND THE TRUMPETS

*Westbeth and a*
*National Breakthrough for the Arts*

Westbeth Artists Housing was a trailblazing project of thirteen connected buildings overlooking the Hudson on the Lower West Side, which became the largest publicly and privately subsidized artists housing project in the nation and the biggest conversion of an industrial building to residential use.[1] It fills a whole square block. It was a milestone on many levels, and Joan shepherded the project to fruition over extraordinary hurdles.[2] It was the largest hands-on project undertaken by the Fund.

Westbeth (located at West Street and Bethune Street) was the first big project for Joan, and she still remembers it as a huge responsibility—both challenging and satisfying. It had started under J.M., who was already funding small artist co-ops, community-based anti-poverty efforts, and housing programs. His own history had a significant impact on many of the projects he supported early on, which aimed to help people struggling economically. "He liked being generous because he knew what being poor is," noted J.M.'s late son, Richard, in a 2014 interview with Liz McEnaney.[3] The smartest thing he did, added Richard, "was marry my mother [Alice]. She was a cultured girl from European parents" who had a great interest in art. She brought art into the Kaplan household and brought J.M. into the worlds of art and music. All four Kaplan children, in different ways, developed a strong affinity for the arts. Westbeth clearly fit the family's interests.

Artists' studios had been disappearing around the city with the widespread clearance that started after World War II. Greenwich Village was, of course, world famous as an artists' enclave, once filled with the sunlit garrets that enabled bursts of show-stopping creativity. In 1965, Roger L. Stevens—a theater producer, real estate executive, and friend of J.M.'s—was appointed by President John F. Kennedy as the founding chairman of the Kennedy Center for the Performing Arts in 1961, and then by President Lyndon B. Johnson to be the first head of the new National Endowment for the Arts (NEA) in 1965. (The arts of all kinds got serious attention during the Kennedy and Johnson administrations.) Westbeth was Stevens's brainchild.

One of Stevens's early NEA initiatives was a survey of the arts nationwide. Among his revelations was that live-work space—lofts where artists could both live and work—was scarce and diminishing, even though the need was great for artists and their families. Clearly, Stevens realized, without studio or living space, there could be no arts, since artists of all kinds struggled to find both. Westbeth was conceived as a model for subsidized artists' housing. "Roger understood what

Westbeth Artists Housing was formerly a Bell Telephone Laboratories complex, with the New York Central Railroad elevated railway going through it.
CREDIT: COURTESY AT&T ARCHIVES AND HISTORY CENTER

was needed. When he came up with this idea, he thought of it as national. But, he insisted, New York—it had to be in New York! He rather naturally turned to my father, his fellow New Yorker, old friend, and earlier partner in real estate ventures," Joan recalled in an interview.

The nearby area now famously known as SoHo was slowly turning into an artists' enclave for those who could scrape together a few dollars and persuade landlords to let them illegally occupy lofts in empty industrial buildings zoned for manufacturing. Owners were just waiting for their buildings to be condemned for the long-planned Lower Manhattan Expressway (known as LOMEX), which would have demolished forty-five acres of five- to six-story factory buildings (no higher than a hook-and-ladder fire truck could reach) in this area just south of Greenwich Village. Four hundred and sixteen buildings, two thousand housing units, and at least eight hundred commercial

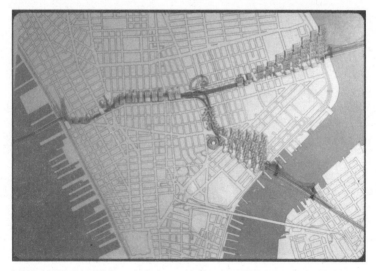

Map of Robert Moses's proposed Lower Manhattan Expressway, which would have wiped out SoHo, Chinatown, and much of Greenwich Village

and industrial buildings were in the path of the expressway. So, too, were neighboring Little Italy and Chinatown. Many businesses had already moved away due to the uncertainty and instability.[4]

The proposal for a ten-lane expressway lined with huge apartment towers—which would link Long Island to the rest of the country—had been born in the 1940s but was being vigorously fought in the 1960s. This was one of Moses's pet highway projects. It seemed only a matter of time before it would be built. Defeating highway proposals at that time was unthinkable, as was installing new tenants in empty buildings. What business would move into a doomed building? Functional ones stood under-occupied or empty, but not because they were structurally unsound or unsuitable for productive use.[5] Artists had started filling the empty spaces illegally, generating the transformation of this significant, cast-iron-filled, industrial neighborhood that became known as SoHo. The neighborhood's renewal inspired and accelerated the slow rebirth of downtowns that, before SoHo emerged, was happening primarily in residential row-house neighborhoods around the country.

The idea of a legal and publicly subsidized conversion of an industrial building into artists' live-work spaces was relatively new. Before working with Stevens, J.M. and the Fund had supported several small-scale artist-studio conversions. For example, as the *New York Times* reported, "in 1963-7, two red brick buildings on Greenwich and West 12th Streets, that had once been the warehouses for an iron foundry, were converted into New York City's first low-income housing cooperative for artists, with twelve units of live-work space."[6]

Kaplan and Stevens had partnered on a small project to convert a five-story loft building at Spring and Mercer to be run as a nonprofit.[7] (This became artist Donald Judd's home and eventually the site of his foundation.) So when Stevens came up with the larger concept for Westbeth as affordable housing for artists, J.M. responded immediately. The project was an enormous risk on many levels: nothing like it had ever been done before, and they needed to overcome zoning rules as well as long-standing thinking and policies, all of which could easily defeat a less resolute team. But both men were already risk-takers in their varied endeavors and shared a determination to overcome seemingly insurmountable barriers. Stevens had the idea to tap into federal funding programs and eventually got the Federal Housing Administration (FHA) to ease its strict guidelines, to allow for the flexible space and large open floors that define a loft. This was the first time that the FHA used its moderate-income housing program for housing for a specific group.

Kaplan and Stevens spent a good deal of time scouring the city for the right site. Joan described, with admiration and good humor, how they "went chasing all around New York City, these two old geezers, looking for the ideal building. . . . They hiked up and climbed down. They went under and over, and yes, it was the two of them."[8] They finally selected the thirteen-building complex in the far west of Greenwich Village that had once belonged to Bell Telephone Laboratories, one of the world's most important research centers. Approximately four thousand scientists and engineers had worked at this imposing space overlooking the Hudson River.

It was in this complex that early radio and radar technology, the first talking movie, the condenser microphone, the first TV broadcast, and the first binary computer were demonstrated. By the mid-1960s, however, not only had Bell Labs outgrown the facility, but the noise and vibrations from passing traffic made certain experiments impossible. The company moved to a new suburban complex in Holmdel, New Jersey, designed by Eero Saarinen. The empty property was brought to the attention of Kaplan and Stevens by the prominent New York developer William Zeckendorf, who was expecting to be the developer for the nearby proposed West Village urban renewal plan, which was eventually defeated by the local community, led by Jane Jacobs, after a long fight.

Inland of the building was the unused elevated rail line that the Fund had once supported as a restored railway. Blocking its view of the Hudson on the other side was the elevated West Side Highway.[9] Joan recalled that the neighborhood was a dead zone, "a wilderness and a bit frightening at night, even." The nascent SoHo loft movement had not yet come that far west.

Not only was the vicinity a backwater, but the idea of adaptive reuse was brand new. The 1833 Jefferson Market Courthouse at Sixth and Greenwich Avenues reopened as a branch library in 1967, an early win for a neighborhood-preservation group led by the indefatigable Margot Gayle. That historic preservation victory was of a very different type than what Stevens and Kaplan were trying to achieve with Westbeth. But ad hoc projects in other cities—like San Francisco's Ghirardelli Square (a former chocolate factory) and Seattle's Pike Place Market (a farmers' market threatened by urban renewal)—were opening in the late 1960s, thereby spotlighting the creative re-use of old industrial and commercial buildings. However, none of these similar projects had the singular focus of creating affordable artists' housing.

While finding and securing the site was not easy, it was clear that the biggest challenges were yet to come. "The questions were endless," Joan recalled. "Who was this for exactly? What did we mean by artists? Which disciplines to include? Just painters, sculptors—the first plan—or a broader range? How to choose them? We argued and discussed and in the end concluded that Westbeth had to be for all the arts and for artists in different stages of their career, such as new and aspiring or successful and mature. We wanted sculptors and painters of course but also dancers and composers, theater people and musicians, photographers and writers. We had no idea yet as to who, or how to find them." Joan put together a committee of cultural leaders in the city, including heads of museums and other art institutions. "We asked ourselves, 'What will be the character of this new place?'" The committee established the criteria.

As Joan pointed out, "No one was willing to presume to make critical assessment of the work; this was, after all, about housing, not awards. But they did determine that residents would have to be serious, full-time artists, as distinct from 'Sunday painters,' within all disciplines." There was an interesting additional level to the requirements. "The usual preference," Joan said, "was for the deeper creative within the discipline—say, the playwright before the actor, the choreographer before the dancer, the composer before the performer, and so on." The goal was for maximum diversity of people—singles and families,

Interior living space in Westbeth
CREDIT: EZRA STOLLER/ESTO

and different races, ages, genders, and backgrounds, as well as
art disciplines and styles—in hopes of creating a normal, happily functioning, vital New York community. Many of those
fortunate earliest Westbeth residents still live and work there.

Of course, there was the actual conversion of the property.
A young, then-unknown architect, Richard Meier—a friend
of Richard Kaplan—was selected as the designer. Up to that
point, no architects had a track record with adaptive reuse. Joan
recalled that "Richard said, 'Well, there was this bright kid in
my class at Harvard Design School.' We interviewed him and
we liked him. And we said, 'What the heck! Let's give him a
shot.' . . . It was so informal, I have to admit, the way we did
things then."[10] Richard, also an architect, told Meier that "it

was not appropriate for the developer's son to be the designer," good as he might have been.[11]

Meier had recently opened his office and designed two houses. Previously, he had worked in the office of famed Bauhaus-trained architect Marcel Breuer.[12] Since then, Meier has become one of the world's most prestigious architects and a Pritzker Architecture Prize winner, the youngest at the time. Ironically, almost fifty years later, Meier also designed three predominantly glass-faced, luxury apartment houses two-and-a-half blocks south of Westbeth, for which two loft buildings were demolished.

In a 2016 interview in his signature white-on-white-style office in a Tenth Avenue loft building, Meier explained that a project like Westbeth had never been legally done, yet "the city had changed the laws making loft living legal." Nevertheless, it was "more complex" than imaginable today. "Everything had to be changed," he noted, or worked out in new ways, such as building codes that required two means of egress. The city council had passed special legislation, and a complicated funding package—private, federal, city, and bank financing—was arranged.

"We worked day and night with many unexpected problems," Meier said. "No one had renovated an industrial building this size. One warehouse project in London had been converted, but the idea of large-scale lofts was new. Joan was involved every step of the way, especially in making sure the community of artists included a mixture of painters, sculptors, dancers, and others."

Joan, by then vice president of the Fund, carried the ball forward, "on time and on budget," she noted proudly. She was very committed to the idea of an expanded definition of who is an artist, and of a diverse, NYC-appropriate community at Westbeth. She worked with Meier, architect Tod Williams in Meier's office, and construction manager Dixon Bain to finish in two years. She persuaded city officials to pass the first special zoning district, which permitted live-work space in an industrial zone. She, like her mother, Alice, as indicated earlier, had long shown a strong interest in the arts and had helped get the American Folk Art Museum off the ground and start the American Federation of Arts.[13]

Stevens and Kaplan had hoped Westbeth would be a model—and it was, but in many different variations. One immediate consequence, as described by Columbia professor Andrew Dolkart, was "the transformation of the abandoned Chickering & Sons piano factory in Boston into artists' live/ work space which was undertaken as a direct result of the success of the New York project. . . . It is clear that the general success of Westbeth and the national publicity that it received were a catalyst for other conversions of urban industrial buildings into artists' housing."[14] Critics in many publications extolled Westbeth's virtues from different angles. Ada Louise Huxtable in the *New York Times* proclaimed that "no trumpets sounded when Westbeth triumphed over the system, but they should have," since Westbeth's open apartment plans "represent a first step out of the steel trap of FHA rules, one of the most powerful and deadly impediments of domestic design."[15]

She noted that "important ground has been broken at West-beth and valuable lessons learned."

In 1977, architect Carmi Bee had received a grant from the NEA to do a national study of artists' workspace, "Where Artists Live." The result was dismaying, with most living in "grubby, seedy places" in downtowns in Seattle, San Francisco, Los Angeles, Chicago, and Boston. The study caught the eye of struggling Salt Lake City artist Stephen A. Goldsmith, who had already read about Westbeth and was inspired. "I was desperately in need of workspace I could afford," he said in an interview. He had been living in unheated warehouses with no running water and had to keep moving as short-term leases ran out. He knew other artists in similar straits. "SoHo had already become chic," but Westbeth was a different and more applicable model, because, Goldsmith added, "we were mindful of not trying to be chic." A safe, affordable workspace was the goal.

Inspired by Westbeth, Goldsmith converted his first building, the Pierpont Project, and included artists, an acting company, a clothing manufacturer, an antique store, offices, a bookstore of the American Institute of Architects, and a consignment furniture store. The long-term result? Five affordable, nonprofit, co-op conversions of industrial buildings in Salt Lake City with three hundred units. Arts-related commercial tenants occupy the ground floors where possible to help subsidize the residential artists. The diverse assortment of tenants at street-level have created a mini local economy.[16] All over the country—like in the environs of Westbeth and SoHo—neighborhoods and downtowns organically reemerged as vibrant city districts as loft conversions spread.

At the time, Westbeth was not thought of or labeled as a historic preservation project.[17] The Landmarks Law had been passed in 1965, but its application was weak and historic buildings were still falling needlessly. A vigorous campaign to designate the cast-iron buildings in SoHo as a historic district was being waged by Margot Gayle, who had founded Friends of Cast Iron Architecture with J.M. Kaplan Fund support, but SoHo was not officially designated a historic district until 1973. (An extension to the district was added in 2010.) With the rebuilding of the West Side Highway and creation of Hudson River Park, Westbeth is now noticed but not necessarily understood by many more people. The surrounding far-west corner of Greenwich Village is more vibrant than ever. But affordable housing for anybody, especially artists, is increasingly out of reach.

Today, Joan doesn't believe the significance of the Westbeth accomplishment is adequately recognized. "It's rather taken for granted," she said. Carmi Bee, former chair of the Westbeth board of directors, concurred in a 2016 interview: "The enormity of its significance is unrecognized. It broke all the rules and helped legitimize the idea of live-work space for artists. It paralleled what was happening in SoHo but its impact went beyond New York."[18] As Joan wrote in the first Westbeth newsletter:

> Westbeth is public housing that, because of the unique circumstances of its origin, its special purpose and unconventional methods of operation, is a social experiment of enormous importance to this country. At stake here are large

issues about the obligation of the slow-moving federal bu-
reaucracy to respond to human need; about the possibilities
for people to form and govern their own living and working environment; and about the very nature and meaning of
community—community of artists, specifically; all communities by implication.

In the beginning, J.M., Stevens, and Joan had no idea the
sheer number of roadblocks that would eventually confront
them. The project broke every rule in the book. Special zoning was needed to allow living and working space in the same
building, let alone same unit. This was the era when "separate
uses" was believed to be the correct zoning model—the antith-
esis, of course, of vibrant, mixed-use urban neighborhoods that
had been the norm before World War II. The city needed to
provide a tax abatement. J.M.'s financial clout was needed to
secure a mortgage from a reluctant bank. State building codes
did not allow for wall-less, open spaces. In fact, to pacify regula-
tors and solve this problem, Meier inserted dashed lines on the
drawings where walls would normally be. Even exposed pipes
and hallway ceilings painted bright colors were novel ideas.

The original intent was to give artists and their families five
years to stabilize and move on, but this was never officially
designated, and hence has been generally ignored. In the end,
384 subsidized units with great natural light and twelve-foot
ceilings were created for artists of all disciplines and stages of
their career. The buildings include large and small commercial
spaces, performance and rehearsal spaces, and artists' studios.
It remains the largest project of its kind in the United States.[19]

# 4

## NO MORE BITES

*Historic Preservation Comes of Age*

Policymakers would be wise to consider John Kenneth Galbraith's 1980 statement: "The preservation movement has one great curiosity. There is never retrospective controversy or regret. Preservationists are the only people in the world who are invariably confirmed in their wisdom after the fact."[1]

I n the 1970s, the seeds of the rebirth of American cities were not always visible, but nevertheless were slowly sprouting among the ruins.[2] By all standard measurements, the '70s were New York's, and most American cities', lowest point and the height of white flight—the exodus of white residents to the suburbs. The idea of flight needs to be rethought. Many residents were pushed out of cities when their neighborhoods were undermined or demolished; only some of them left willingly. Many middle-class occupants of neighborhoods that Robert Moses declared slums may have had no intention of leaving.[3] But by the 1970s, almost three million white people had left, replaced by an influx of African Americans and Hispanics. The

1950s and '60s had seen a loss of about five hundred thousand white residents per year as part of an overall diminishment of the population, as more and more neighborhoods were cleared out and bulldozed and the appeal of the suburbs strengthened. Scrutiny of the displacement figures during urban renewal in a number of targeted neighborhoods in the five boroughs leads to a projection of at least one million people displaced (out of a citywide population of eight million) under slum clearance.

Fueling the exodus was the unspoken national policy of urban dispersal that evolved after World War II.[4] A set of policies favored all the elements that undermined cities: bigger highways, shopping malls, and suburban tract housing. Manufacturing and corporate headquarters were also lured to suburban sites. Redlining by banks and insurance companies made city home ownership untenable, and blockbusting scared homeowners out of otherwise stable neighborhoods. It has been argued, with some validity, that negative city policies—not external forces or national policies—prompted the exodus of residents and businesses from inner cities. This is a half-truth that omits the most important half: cheap land, low taxes, scores of federal funding programs for first-time home buyers and veterans, insured mortgages, and subsidies for water and sewer connections all lured residents and businesses to the suburbs. The suburban dream of home ownership was a formidable draw. Suburbanization became national policy. Only later could that departure be called urban flight—flight from urban frustrations like diminished city services, failing infrastructure, and crime.

At the same time, Americans had fallen in love with the automobile. The automobile was as much a reflection of status and style as it was an answer to the needs of an increasingly mobile society. Ada Louise Huxtable summed it up nicely in a 1976 *New York Times* article entitled "The Fall and Rise of Main Street." "A mobile society that had established a new set of rituals forced passage to the 'climate controlled' covered shopping mall in all of its frigid, canned-music-drenched, plastic glamour," she writes. "On old streets, old buildings were torn down for parking lots, in a bleak, gap-toothed kind of mutilation. Main Street had become a sad, shabby relic, empty shopfronts alternating with faded displays that looked as if time had stopped on one of those 1940s summer afternoons."[5] Nationally, the 1970s also saw the oil embargo, which sent the national economy and local budgets into a tailspin and challenged car-dependent lifestyles.

Things were bad, yet 1970 also had the first national Earth Day, and within a few years the Clean Air and Clean Water Acts were passed under President Richard M. Nixon. The bicentennial tall ships event gave the city a new glow. In the same year, the country began to rethink urban potential when Americans watched the extraordinary opening of the Faneuil Hall/ Quincy Market in downtown Boston. The common wisdom was that downtowns were dead, until people woke up to the extraordinary draw of the "festival marketplace." Similar projects were opening in San Francisco. The innovative reuse of historic landmarks made thousands rethink the indiscriminate losses incurred by new-only rebuilding policies.

There is no doubt, however, that New York and cities across the country were facing serious challenges. When many saw NYC as a lost cause, Joan believed in it. This is critical to understand how the seeds of a positive future were nurtured by philanthropies like the J.M. Kaplan Fund.[6] As Joan recalled, "I hung out with [JM] in his office, as he ate his daily apple with peanut butter." She was her father's "support system, really. And I had become involved in the substantive issues." She can't recall specifically how she got interested in historic preservation. "It just seemed like breathing, it was so natural. I was on the Municipal Art Society, architecture and design groups, and all those city issues. So I kind of introduced J.M. to the preservation scene just because I so believed in those groups and their valiant efforts."

The return-to-the-city movement had started slowly in the 1960s in the brownstone neighborhoods of Park Slope in Brooklyn and the Upper West Side. When my husband and I bought our brownstone in 1967, by definition and without even knowing it we were preservationists. But the motivation was finding an appealing place to live at an affordable price. House tours were revealing how well and how relatively inexpensively one could live in the city and still have a backyard. As new people, often young families, started moving into partially empty neighborhoods, block parties and block associations started forming. These groups were not necessarily concerned with preservation at first but about security, garbage collection, and other quality-of-life issues. (Eventually, this gradual movement heated up and led to the gentrification that has been such a troubling issue ever since.) The preservation agenda spread citywide. SoHo's popularity was increasing rapidly, and its formal landmark designation came in 1973. Across the country, magazines and newspapers featured articles on city living, in both brownstones and lofts.

Row of brownstones in the Park Slope Historic District
CREDIT: HISTORIC DISTRICTS COUNCIL

## THE PRESERVATION
## MOVEMENT EXPANDS

In the 1970s, New York City's preservation movement was emerging in a new form. The Landmarks Law had been passed in 1965, though in a very weak form: operable only for six months every three years, with no provisions for designating interiors, landscapes, or city-owned properties. Local preservation battles were going on all over the city, and the preservation community was slowly converging. At first, several of these new organizations started as committees of the Municipal Art Society, encouraged by then MAS director Kent Barwick, before becoming independent and receiving funding from the J.M. Kaplan Fund and the Vincent Astor Foundation. The Historic Districts Council (HDC), founded in 1970, was one of the first and started as an MAS committee. Member groups represented the fourteen designated historic districts and advocated for more political and financial support from the Landmarks Preservation Commission. HDC was an important committee, as citizen groups all over the city were organizing to advocate for historic-district status for their neighborhood. HDC soon changed its focus to advocate for designation of neighborhoods around the five boroughs and became independent in 1985, with Fund support.

A number of committed preservationists, mostly on the board or involved with MAS, were focusing on expanding the impact of preservation during these years, and the Fund— often in partnership with the Vincent Astor Foundation, the New York Foundation, and others—was ready to financially support each effort.[7] As Tony Wood described, "There was a realization that with the hardship clause in the law, we would continue to lose buildings unless somebody knew how to really develop an expertise and acumen in saving white elephant buildings in the time period before the festival marketplace.[8] So the New York Landmarks Conservancy was created to be this group of preservationists. It was meant to have real technical abilities at a level MAS wouldn't." The Landmarks Conservancy's mission was to find new uses for the buildings it fought to save from the wrecking ball.

The group was a significant new addition to the still nascent preservation movement. *New Yorker* writer Brendan Gill was the conservancy's first president and the city's most effective preservation advocate.[9] Also an active board member of MAS, Gill was probably the best known and most significant early advocate of historic preservation in the city. For sixty years, until his death in 1997, Gill wrote profiles, Talk of the Town pieces, theater reviews, and, importantly, architecture articles for the *New Yorker* as the successor to Lewis Mumford's Skyline column.[10] Through his writing and impressive Rolodex of well-connected people, Gill brought the preservation cause into the living rooms and offices of high-powered New Yorkers, summoning their checkbooks for the cause as well. "A man of action, a tireless and articulate campaigner for historic preservation, architectural excellence and the quality of city life," wrote *New York Times* architecture critic Herbert Muschamp when Gill died at the age of eighty-three.

"He was able to call and engage anyone and everyone," said Laurie Beckelman, who served at the conservancy's executive director and later as chair of the Landmarks Preservation Commission. "We wouldn't have gotten where we did without him."

The buildings the conservancy was able to save in the early and mid-1970s were formidable landmarks. The group's first project was the 1902 US Custom House at Bowling Green, designed by Cass Gilbert. This extraordinary beaux arts palace sits at the foot of Broadway and is that major street's visual anchor. It had been the longtime home of the US Customs Service, which moved to the World Trade Center in 1973. It took two decades of hit-and-miss ideas before the Smithsonian's National Museum of the American Indian moved in, in 1994, with some space still used by the US Customs Service.

The Fraunces Tavern block—nineteenth-century commercial buildings in Lower Manhattan that had been scheduled for demolition—was saved, purchased by the Landmarks Conservancy and sold to a developer for conversion to residential and commercial uses. Soon after, an empty, massive, 1899 red-brick Romanesque revival structure, the Archive Building in Greenwich Village, was taken over by the conservancy, which found a developer to convert it into apartments. These projects, Wood explained, "were symbolic of the kind of hardship that landmark designation would not be enough to save. This was early in the 1970s because the law was just kicking in." Today, historic buildings of considerable scale are recognized as economically viable development opportunities by many experienced preservation developers—but in the 1970s, skepticism reigned.

## HISTORIC PRESERVATION SPURS
## NEIGHBORHOOD REVIVAL

Preservation made great strides in the 1970s. While the core of the activist movement was based in Brooklyn Heights, Greenwich Village, and the Upper East Side, the decade saw a rapid increase in mobilization among small and large groups all over Manhattan south of 125th Street and across Brooklyn. Advancing the cause was never easier than with low real estate prices and a developer community less aggressive than it is today. Families and small developers bought and restored dwellings citywide, especially brownstones and single-family homes in Park Slope, Flatbush, the Upper West Side, Chelsea, and Queens.

Marcel Breuer's proposed tower to be built over Grand Central. The Landmarks Preservation Commission's denial of the permit to build brought on the transformative lawsuit that reached the US Supreme Court.

CREDIT: GRAND CENTRAL AIR RIGHTS BUILDING, PROPOSAL DRAWING, MARCEL BREUER PAPERS, 1920–1986, ARCHIVES OF AMERICAN ART, SMITHSONIAN INSTITUTION

It is fair to say that the spotlight on the value of old, neglected, and inexpensive residential properties fueled the city's rebirth. The experts had not yet given up on their opinion that cities were dead and the suburbs were the place to raise a family. But young families had started questioning the conventional wisdom, turning that notion into action when they

71

discovered the value available in historic buildings in the city. This would accelerate in the 1980s and '90s, when interest in New York real estate development picked up in new ways and neighborhoods felt safer.

The biggest boost to preservation came when New York's Landmarks Law was upheld by the US Supreme Court in 1978. A few years before, Judge Irving H. Saypol of New York's State Supreme Court had ruled in favor of Penn Central, which had sued the city to overturn the designation of Grand Central Terminal. The Landmarks Preservation Commission had denied Penn Central its application to build a tower over Grand Central, and the state court had awarded Penn Central, owner of the terminal, $60 million in damages. That was a hefty sum for a financially strapped city in the mid-1970s, and there was talk within the administration of then mayor Abraham Beame of de-designating the 1913 terminal to satisfy the judgment against the city. Undoubtedly, this would have meant the end of individual landmark designations and, possibly, of historic districts too. MAS was pushing the city to continue the fight up the legal chain to uphold the law, letting the mayor know that it considered this a life-and-death issue.

While the administration debated the issue internally, MAS and Kent Barwick mounted a public relations campaign to pressure the mayor to fight for the terminal and the law as vigorously as possible. MAS opened a street-level storefront on 45th Street just off Madison Avenue, distributing literature, buttons ("No more bites out of the Big Apple"), ties with apples on them, and other such items. The storefront was funded by the J.M. Kaplan Fund, already a longtime, generous MAS supporter. At the same time, Barwick put together a gold-plated group of prominent city residents, the Citizens Committee to Save Grand Central, and devised a legal strategy to appeal the expected negative decision that came in February 1975. The decision was on the front page of the *New York Times*.

One phone call changed everything. "I will never forget that day as long as I live," recalled Laurie Beckelman, an MAS staff member at the time, in conversation. "I spent the day sitting in this tiny office answering a phone that never stopped ringing. A woman called and asked to speak to Kent Barwick. She claimed to be Jackie Onassis. I was sure it was a prank, but Kent took the call." It was indeed Mrs. Onassis offering her help. She joined the committee and eventually the MAS board of directors. She wrote to Mayor Beame: "Is it not cruel to let our city die by degrees, stripped of all her proud monuments, until there will be nothing left of all her history and beauty to inspire our children. If they are not inspired by the past of our city, where will they find the strength to fight for her future?"[11] These words are immortalized on a plaque in the terminal's foyer to the main entrance at 42nd Street and Park Avenue.

"It was the coming out, in a way, for Jackie Onassis in New York. Every magazine in America and Europe knew about Jackie and Grand Central," Beckelman added. In fact, this partnership put historic preservation on the national map as well. There was no turning back; preservation became a nationwide movement.

"Jacqueline Onassis brought to MAS a visceral belief in preservation," writes Gregory F. Gilmartin.[12] "But more important, she attracted news cameras as a flame draws moths.

People hesitated to rebuff her. They took her phone calls. Even Abe Beame was susceptible."

Beckelman observed what many others have assumed: in the end, "a nicely placed phone call from Jackie may have been what finally convinced the mayor to file the appeal."

## JACKIE

Because Jackie agreed to participate in the MAS-organized "Landmark Express" Amtrak train ride from New York to DC, it got tremendous TV and press attention. In Washington, a press conference was planned to bring attention to New York City's lawsuit. Coincidentally, the train ride took place the day before the Supreme Court hearing on the case. MAS had absolutely no prior knowledge of the date the case was scheduled for argument until two days before. As Margot Wellington, former MAS director, explained, "Whitney North Seymour, a prominent board member of MAS, came into my office saying, 'You know, Margot, that one is not allowed to lobby the Supreme Court. I just had lunch with one of the justices and learned that the court hearing will take place the day after your train.' I said, 'Oh, Whitney, do I have to call off the train?' Chuckling, Whitney answered, 'Of course not.'" In the end, the Supreme Court ruled in favor of the city and against the railroad. The Landmarks Law did not deprive Penn Central its use of or income from the terminal. The tower was killed and the Landmarks Law saved and, in fact, made stronger.

These preservation victories came not long after the infamous 1975 *Daily News* headline, "Ford to City: Drop Dead."

President Gerald Ford had cruelly rebuffed the city's appeal for financial aid when bankruptcy was looming. And while the Grand Central victory gave a much-welcomed lift to the city's spirits, it did not change reality. Everything in the city exhibited neglect and decay. Individual homeowners, renovators, and neighborhood activists were not the only ones tackling areas of great need.

To review the J.M. Kaplan Fund's annual reports for the years 1978 and 1979, Joan's first years at the helm, is to find a fascinating and diverse group of citywide and neighborhood-based organizations—not just in Manhattan—taking on the challenges of the era and getting Fund support.[13] The Bronx Museum of the Arts was mounting an exhibition, *Devastation/ Resurrection: The South Bronx*, to celebrate the extraordinary grassroots efforts to rebuild that decimated borough.[14] The Bronx River Restoration Project was trying to clean up the Bronx River and turn it into a community asset, while the Trust for Public Land was conducting workshops to increase community participation in land-use planning. The Staten Island Council on the Arts was trying to save open space in the Stapleton neighborhood, and the Citizens Committee for New York City was working to create one hundred new block associations.

## PRESERVATION IS ABOUT URBANISM

Preservation is never about historic buildings alone; it is about urbanism, preserving the whole city—which is simply the sum of its diverse and very interconnected parts—building new to fit comfortably with the old, respecting the existing scale, and

75

disallowing the overwhelming scale that over powers and destroys neighborhoods. Jane Jacobs said it was about balancing the urban ecology. The Fund grants in this era display the grassroots ways people were coming together on so many fronts to take on the challenges of a city that had seen better days. The well-known New York Shakespeare Festival, the Brooklyn Children's Museum, and the Brooklyn Academy of Music were all playing their part to increase the city's appeal, while lesser-known groups like the Academy of American Poets, the Center for Book Arts, and the Jargon Society were doing the kind of only-in-New-York things that proved that the city might be down but it was clearly not out—and the Fund was there with support. The Fund was not alone in giving to these efforts, but it was invariably early in the door and strategically important. Creativity was surging, despite the endless hardships that overwhelmed many. The Fund embraced a long list of civil liberties initiatives, including the Asian American Legal Defense Fund, the Ms. Foundation, Planned Parenthood, and the New York Civil Liberties Union. The Center for National Policy Review, the Children's Cultural Foundation, and Catalyst, Inc., were not household names, but their respective leaders had come up with a creative idea that inspired Fund support.

In the realm of parks and open spaces, a variety of groups were tackling those amenities recognized today as so critical to a livable city. The Horticultural Society of New York was taking on community gardens. The Green Guerillas, as we will see, were expanding their flower gardens and restoration work in public parks. The Parks Council (now New Yorkers for Parks) was focused on Bryant and Riverside Parks. The Street Tree Consortium was mounting a fundraising campaign to plant and maintain more city trees. The Greensward Foundation was trying to protect and preserve Central Park. The Central Park Community Fund brought together various groups focused on Central Park to coordinate planning and actions. Out of several of the Central Park efforts emerged the Central Park Conservancy, first headed by Elizabeth Barlow Rogers, who had been appointed by parks commissioner Gordon Davis as the first Central Park administrator and whose first salary, Davis said, was paid for by the Fund.

It was never smooth sailing for the historic preservation movement, no matter how often it was shown how preservation enhances the physical, social, cultural, and economic fabric of cities everywhere—yes, everywhere—big and small. Those who measure the overall health of a place by the number of new and bigger buildings always attempt to challenge this reality. In New York City, real estate interests were looking for a way to overcome or get around the limits that preservation imposed on less than 3 percent then—still less than 4 percent now—of the city's property.[15] They continue to vigorously thwart preservation efforts.

## RELIGIOUS PROPERTIES: A NATIONAL CHALLENGE

The momentum of the Grand Central victory—huge as it was—did not last long before a new challenge emerged. This new battle was tricky, because it involved religious properties

Saint Bartholomew's Church on Park Avenue wanted to demolish the parish house and open space (R) to make room for new office tower. Formidable citywide opposition, led by MAS, prevented that from happening.

CREDIT: EDMUND VINCENT GILLON. MUSEUM OF THE CITY OF NEW YORK. 2013.3.2.1822

and the challengers tried to pit preservation against feeding the poor and the homeless. Predictably, Joan immediately joined the struggle with her energy and funding. Also prominently involved was the Vincent Astor Foundation. Saint Bartholomew's Episcopal Church, housed at 50th Street and Park Avenue in a 1916 jewel of Byzantine revival design by Bertram Goodhue, proposed in 1984 to tear down its six-story community house and replace it with a fifty-nine-story office building.

The community house was architecturally of a piece with the church, and both were designated landmarks. The church justified its decision by citing the expense of maintaining the elaborate structure and fulfilling its mission. The Vestry of Saint Bartholomew's challenged in court the constitutionality of the landmark designation of religious properties on the grounds of the division of church and state, but lost the challenge.[16] A hardship provision already in the Landmarks Law afforded some measure of relief to religious properties before the Saint Bart's challenge. One synagogue, in nonreligious ownership, on the Upper West Side had been demolished with the Landmarks Preservation Commission's approval.

Undaunted, the city's religious establishment sought relief from the state legislature in Albany. A measure to exempt houses of worship across the state from local preservation laws was introduced. A concerted battle ensued that included Jackie Onassis, the Municipal Art Society, the Landmarks Conservancy, the Preservation League of New York State, assorted local groups, and the city's political leadership, headed by then mayor Ed Koch. While successful in killing the state legislation, the preservation community knew it had to more thoroughly address the religious properties' challenge, beyond the public debate.

This legislative fight in New York was a wake-up call for the national preservation community. Religious properties in every community carry unique benefits and burdens, and they don't have private investors to depend on for the heavy maintenance and restoration challenges that come with architectural gems. Recognition was widespread in New York and elsewhere that

The rescue and restoration of the 1887 Eldridge Street Synagogue started with grants from the J.M. Kaplan Fund and the Vincent Astor Foundation in 1986.
CREDIT: KATE MILFORD

a way had to be found to help religious properties care for their landmark structures. They all invariably had expensive restoration issues. Restoration of the Eldridge Street Synagogue on the Lower East Side, for example, took approximately twenty years and $20 million dollars, but it gained more than twenty thousand supporters, including local, state, and federal funding. It is now the Museum at Eldridge Street, welcoming

some forty thousand visitors yearly while remaining a synagogue with Sabbath and holiday services.[17]

At the Fund, Joan and staff member Tony Wood were
thinking about creating something concrete to help land-
marked religious properties, as well as to build a base of political support to push back against future efforts that might try
to remove religious properties from landmark protection. They
approached the New York Landmarks Conservancy, whose
technical assistance program for landmark-property owners was
already being generously supported by the Fund. The Landmarks Conservancy, with Fund support, launched the Sacred
Sites Program (Joan picked the name). From then on, religious
properties around New York State have had available grants for
both technical assistance and actual restoration work. "When
we approached the conservancy leadership," recalled Wood,
"they were delighted and already had something like that in
mind but didn't think anyone would fund it. As with much of
what the Fund did, it is fair to say the initiative and some key
leadership came from Kaplan, though the ideas and interest
were already out there in the preservation community."

There was also a larger national conversation going on about
the challenges facing religious properties in Boston, Philadelphia, Detroit, and other places. Out of these conversations,
in which Wood participated on behalf of the Fund, came the
conclusion there needed to be a national organization focused
on this issue, one that would pull together religious leaders
and preservationists. Basing it in New York was out of the
question since so much was already happening there, so in
1986 Philadelphia was chosen as the headquarters for Partners

for Sacred Places, and the J.M. Kaplan Fund was among the early supporters. Partners for Sacred Places provides technical assistance and grants to sacred sites of all kinds, including those with shrinking congregations but whose buildings could be used as a community resource beyond the religious function. "Kaplan was funding both the advocacy around fights like Saint Bartholomew, including church/state issues," Wood observed, "as well as the direct assistance programs—a planned strategy."

The seeds that sprouted in the '70s and flowered in the '80s would grow deep roots and gain broad public recognition. In fact, by the '90s, even the "experts" were acknowledging New York City's turnaround, although without serious recognition of the meaningful contributions of the earlier, localized efforts described in this book. Most of the expert evaluations were that these efforts were too small, too ad hoc, and not meaningful. To this day, most people have no clue where and when these successes started. Most will cite the big projects that came later, many of which would not have even happened if the earlier smaller projects hadn't paved the way. New construction in most neighborhoods did not occur until grassroots efforts demonstrated a viable market.

Today, for example, Greenmarkets around the city are taken for granted (as we will see in Chapter 6). The first Greenmarket grant came from the J.M. Kaplan Fund in 1976 without any big study beforehand. The markets were an instant hit. By 1986, support for nineteen Greenmarkets around the city was included in a Fund grant to the Council on the Environment. The city's big parks were also getting increased attention: for example, the Central Park Conservancy, Prospect Park Alliance, Wave Hill, Riverside Park Fund, and Staten Island Greenbelt. More than a dozen organizations were focusing on local parks in different boroughs, and some were developing local gardens to grow food and encourage healthy diets (Green Guerillas, Parks Council, America the Beautiful Fund, Riverside Park, New York Street Tree Consortium, Bronx Frontier Development Corporation, and Bronx River Restoration Project led by Ruth Anderberg). The list of neighborhood preservation groups had also grown (Friends of the Upper East Side led by Helena Rosenthal, CIVITAS led by Genie Rice, Landmark West! led by Arlene Simon, the Drive to Protect the Ladies' Mile led by Jack Taylor, Pleasant Village Block Association [Harlem], Queensborough Preservation League led by Jeffrey Kroessler, Saint Nicholas Neighborhood Preservation, and Housing Rehabilitation Corporation). The historic preservation movement was in full swing—as always, supported by the Fund and often by the Vincent Astor Foundation as well. Preservation had become more specialized (for example, Friends of Terra Cotta, led by Susan Tunick) and individual restoration efforts were proliferating (such as the Gracie Mansion Conservancy, in part founded and headed by Joan).

By the 1980s, the J.M. Kaplan Fund's interests and investments around the state had increased as well. There was the heritage task force for the Hudson River Valley, preservation of the Wilderstein estate (with its Tiffany interiors and a Calvert Vaux landscape), Pete Seeger's Hudson River sloop *Clearwater* as a floating environmental center, the Hudson

Riverkeeper Fund to monitor water pollution law compliance, and both Scenic Hudson and Open Space Institute, preeminent watchdog organizations long on Kaplan funding lists. The Adirondack Land Trust and Adirondack Wild protected threatened land upstate. Like downstate interests, the Fund's upstate focus included protecting open land, historic preservation, the Hudson Valley as a connected whole, and, of course, the river that so defines this major section of New York State.

When you look at this extraordinary array of bottom-up efforts—only some of the initiatives on the Fund's agenda—it is easy to see how a city can pull itself up from the gutter to create a livable, vibrant, urban complex. Many funders joined in support. And with judiciously placed grants around the state, it is also easy to see how this assortment of distinct efforts connected to preserve and strengthen the larger built and natural environment of New York State.

## THE STORIES ARE ENDLESS

Action and printed words reinforce one another in multiple situations. This was certainly true with historic preservation advocacy, invariably advanced by serious publications supported by the Fund. In fact, few efforts in the city's historic preservation movement did not have an early Fund-sponsored book to introduce and advance their cause. "Those books were critical for the launch of a new effort," noted Tony Wood. Examples abound.

*End of the Road for Ladies' Mile?* by Margaret Moore helped begin the successful campaign to designate the Ladies' Mile

Historic
Preservation
in Queens

Jeffrey A. Kroessler and Nina S. Rappaport
Queensborough Preservation League

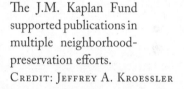

The J.M. Kaplan Fund
supported publications in
multiple neighborhood-
preservation efforts.
CREDIT: JEFFREY A. KROESSLER

Historic District, the stretch of Sixth Avenue from 15th Street
to 23rd Street lined with late-nineteenth-century department
stores. Up until the 1920s, this was the fashion street. Once on
the brink of widespread demolition, the Drive to Protect the
Ladies' Mile District advocated vigorously for these buildings'
designation as landmarks. The former stores, once declared ob-
solete by developers intent on tearing them down, now serve
their original purpose again as retail stores or malls. The book
came out in 1986; the Landmarks Preservation Commission
designated the historic district in 1989.

*A Dream Fulfilled: City and Suburban's York Avenue Estate* by
Andrew Dolkart and Sharon Z. Macosko was published by the
Coalition to Save City and Suburban Housing, Inc. That ef-
fort aimed to preserve the square block of eighteen beige-brick

model tenements developed in 1913 by a group of wealthy New Yorkers—including John Jacob Astor IV—who were willing to limit the return on their investment. The six-story walk-ups were the first public housing projects of their kind. The book helped galvanize support to landmark that complex and was important for the successful legal challenge that followed. Both the Fund and the Vincent Astor Foundation supported that effort, led by Betty Cooper Wallerstein, to prevent prominent developer Peter Kalikow from demolishing the buildings.

*The Texture of Tribeca*, written by Andrew Dolkart for the Tribeca Community Association in 1989, was part of the efforts to get historic-district designation for Tribeca (short for "the triangle below Canal Street"). This area on the Lower West Side bordering the waterfront had been a center for produce shipping, dry-goods production, and textiles, filled with distinctive cast-iron buildings similar to those in SoHo, which is just to the north. With the designation and redevelopment of SoHo, Tribeca became the target for demolition and new construction by developers, threatening the distinctive character of this historic quarter of the city. Four Tribeca historic districts were designated between 1991 and 1992 after years of local effort. A fifth was designated in 2002.

*Landmarks of the Bronx*—also published in 1989, by Gary Hermalyn, Robert Kornfeld, and the Bronx County Historical Society—was part of a Fund-generated effort to focus on land-marking in the Bronx. This book focuses on both designated landmarks—of which there is a rich supply—and the undesignated but proposed historic districts. Amazingly, little has been officially designated along the Grand Concourse, which has the largest concentration of art deco apartment houses in the world but has, for the most part, been overlooked by the Landmarks Preservation Commission—although not by real estate investors.

*Historic Preservation in Queens* by Jeffrey Kroessler and Nina Rappaport was published through the Queensborough Preservation League in 1990 as part of an effort to jump-start preservation in Queens. While Queens is thought of as a predominantly "newer" borough, this book zeroes in on a multitude of worthy individual landmarks and historic districts, only some of which have been designated.

*Jackson Heights: A Garden in the City* by Daniel Karatzas was published the same year with the Jackson Heights Beautification Group as part of a preservation effort. This Queens community had evolved between the two World Wars as a planned, streetcar suburb, with a mix of row houses and six-story apartment houses built around well-landscaped courtyards. The term "garden apartment" emerged at this time, and Jackson Heights was the epitome of it, often in the English country house or mock-Tudor style. Shopping streets were conveniently located within walking distance. A portion of Jackson Heights was designated a historic district in 1993.

*Historic Houses in New York City Parks*, for the Historic House Trust, was published in 1989 and then in 1992 as a second edition. New York has a rich assortment of historic houses, some designated since the book was last published. The Historic House Trust manages twenty-three historic houses in cooperation with the Parks Department. Many people are unaware of how many of these houses exist around the city.

Going statewide in pre-Internet days, the Fund supported the publication of the Preservation League of New York State's 1988 *Preservation Directory: A Guide to Programs, Organizations, and Agencies in New York State* and 1984 *A Fair Land to Build In: The Architecture of the Empire State* by *New Yorker* writer Brendan Gill. Going further into New York State, in 1987 the Fund supported the publication of *Developing a Land Conservation Strategy: A Handbook for Land Trusts* for the Adirondack Land Trust, and in 1991 *Tug Hill Working Lands* by the Tug Hill Commission. *Wilderstein and the Suckleys: A Hudson River Legacy* by Cynthia Owen Philip, published in 2001 for Wilderstein Preservation, was one of many books focusing on the Hudson Valley.

That is the short list of preservation-related publications. Joan had a sharp eye for books that focused on important things that were still unnoticed in the larger world. The preservation, architecture, and landscape books went way beyond the immediacy of a specific local challenge, bringing attention to places and issues that were not yet on many people's radar. They helped spotlight the challenges swirling around architecture, design, and preservation issues, elevating them from the conversations of a few to a robust dialogue across the city.

All these booklets, and more, were underwritten by the Fund, an early expression of Joan's interests in publishing, which took more serious form later on in her program Furthermore, which supports printed and illustrated books.

# 5

# AVOIDING ARMAGEDDON

## *The Battle over Westway and the Theaters*

Two epic controversies unfolded in the 1980s—battles that continue to significantly influence New York City development today. The first was the plan to build Westway: a four-mile, six-lane highway, plus six-lane interior service road (twelve lanes total), on two hundred acres of landfill along and in the Hudson, from 42nd Street down to Battery Park City. The second was the plan to demolish two extraordinary Broadway theaters, the Morosco and the Helen Hayes, to build an atrium-style hotel designed by Atlanta architect John Portman, a building now known as the Marriott Marquis. Both controversies involved history-changing battles of the David and Goliath kind. And both led to precedent-shaping lawsuits that changed development policies. New York is a very different city because of these struggles. The divisions over them were fierce, resulting in friendships disrupted and civic groups bitterly divided.

Many people born in the 1970s and later might not know much about these high-stakes conflicts. Those who lived through them easily forget the reasons for the disputes, let alone their significance. Involved in each controversy, as both a forceful advocate and a major funder, were Joan K. Davidson and the J.M. Kaplan Fund. Although effectively out of the public eye, Joan's support was crucial.

At first, the Save the Theaters effort in the late 1970s and early 1980s narrowly focused on the Helen Hayes and Morosco. Those two incomparable gems were lost, but in the end the remaining historic theaters in the district were officially designated by the city's Landmark Preservation Commission. The theater owners—the same ones who had no interest in seeing the Morosco and Helen Hayes survive—sued to stop the designations. In a significant move, Joan persuaded the Natural Resources Defense Council (NRDC), on whose board she had served for years, to take on the lawsuit. For the first time, the environmental organization embraced the idea that the built environment was as central to environmental conflicts as the natural environment, that the natural and cultural environment were of a piece, and that urban areas were a critical component of the environment. This was the first case to definitively establish that equilibrium.

"We needed legal help," Joan recalled. "I thought of [NRDC cofounder] John Adams, always a miracle worker! NRDC had had no truck with the city, and it was a hard sell for them. 'Heck no, this has nothing to do with NRDC's mission,' some board members said, but somehow John was able to bring his board around. John is my hero and a genius. He signed on NRDC, came to see this as a serious matter, and his people rallied around. After this battle, NRDC officially created its own urban program as a first ever, influencing the entire environmental scene from then on."

As described in a 2017 *New York Times* article, the Westway debate "presented one of the fiercest clashes between environmentalists and development forces the city had ever seen."[1] The case was brought by a coalition of environmentalists, transit advocates, and other civic organizations and was argued, litigated, and decided primarily on environmental grounds. But beyond canceling the proposed highway, this civic argument and resolution marked a turning point in thinking about how New York and cities in general should be developed—whether the car or pedestrians and mass transit should shape and define major policy issues. The Westway fight helped change that conversation both in New York and nationwide. "Westway was an opportunity to get rid of a superhighway—and the idea of a superhighway in a city—and to redirect that money to mass transit," observed Al Butzel, the first lead lawyer for the opposition, in an interview.[2] This fight had a direct impact on similar highway proposals in cities across the country.

Joan, like so many others, took a while to fully understand the complexity and implications of the Westway debate. "I first reacted against it because it would have run right by Westbeth's front door," she recalled, laughing at the simplicity of her initial stance. But she listened to the lawyers and civic opponents, understood the layers of significance and the enormity of the Westway issue, and eventually was a primary funder of the fight. She stayed with it to the end.

Joan's fear of the impact on Westbeth was not irrational. In fact, those quality-of-life considerations applied to the whole stretch of the West Side, since the proposed landfill would have eventually seen super-tall skyscraper development, increased traffic, and environmental damage. "I was persuaded by the lawyers and activists of the urgency of the Westway case," she observed. Both Joan and her father had long cared about the treatment of the Hudson River and, as she recalled, "we had supported early on the Storm King fight [against a power plant upriver (see Chapter 7)], and this was, of course, connected to saving the river in the city too. It was all connected—a conscientiousness about the river, Westbeth, new towers, vehicular traffic, and all that came with it." It took a long time for many members of the public to understand the Westway debate. To this day, many proponents still mourn its defeat.

The most visible and passionate public face of the opposition was a young environmentalist, Marcy Benstock, who was heavily supported by the Fund; Mary Kaplan, Joan's sister, in particular was a big fan of Benstock's. While there was fierce citywide opposition to Westway, proponents and the media often tried to make Benstock the core of the opposition.

The Fund's support for this fight was invaluable, especially because the city's whole power structure—political, social, economic, and media—was pushing for Westway with all available means. The main exceptions included Congressman Ted Weiss and all the West Side elected officials. "Joan helped spread the word and validate the position that it was better to trade in the Westway funds for mass transit than to support a mega real estate deal tied to a highway," Marcy Benstock told me in an interview. Benstock headed and still heads an environmental and public-policy group called the Clean Air Campaign, based in

New York but with a national focus. Benstock and the Clean Air Campaign led the charge against Westway. "Joan helped us by holding a fundraising gathering in her living room with important opponents of Westway present," including John Oakes of the *New York Times*; Adrian DeWind, a prestigious lawyer who later became the head of NRDC's board of litigation committee and then its chairman; and Mitch Bernard, then the lead lawyer for the lawsuit. "Joan totally got it and was able to articulate the issues, and her credibility with her peers helped tremendously in persuading others to support the fight," Benstock added. In the end, Westway was defeated and the existing highway was rebuilt and widened where possible, just as opponents said should happen.

It is easy to oversimplify both the theater and Westway battles, easy to miss how rare, farsighted, and courageous it was to oppose both developments. But when one examines the significance of the conflicts in detail—the extraordinary impediments to stopping such city-changing projects and the powerful forces aligned in their favor—it is even more astonishing. Standing up to power so boldly doesn't happen too often, so when it does, attention must be paid.

## WESTWAY

"There is no question the debate over Westway, in the end, was a plebiscite on mass transit or highways," observed Kent Barwick in an interview. At the time of the controversy, Barwick was not on record supporting or opposing Westway. (Barwick was chair of the Landmarks Preservation Commission from

1976 to 1982 and head of the Municipal Art Society from 1983 to 1995. MAS endorsed Westway.) "It crystallized the issue and strengthened the resolve of transit advocates. The Lower Manhattan Expressway victory was a mere skirmish in comparison; Westway was the Armageddon of highways in the city." Additionally, he noted, "the prolonged Westway debate was a watershed moment, respecting the environment of the river. Until then, rivers were regularly filled in whenever a few more feet of land was desired. Now, a core value is to pay attention to aquatic life."

"The Lower Manhattan Expressway fight was the beginning of the end of the automobile fixation," added Butzel, offering a slightly different view. "Westway expanded the debate. People realized that the lifeline of the city was mass transit, not highways."

Neither Westway nor the theater battle had the editorial board of any newspaper on its side. (At first the *New York Post* opposed the project, but it switched to support.) However, columnists John Oakes and Sydney Schanberg bucked the *New York Times* to convincingly articulate the opposition to both projects. The press liked to focus on the great new parks and development that supposedly would rise on the two hundred acres of Hudson River landfill. The city, however, could not afford to maintain the parks it already had.

Additionally, few Westway proponents foresaw the scale of new buildings that would emerge—much like the super-tall buildings today that, with a tricky manipulation of the zoning, have been rising to disconcerting heights around the city. Some are approaching one hundred stories. The Brooklyn waterfront has been and continues to be transformed in this way because all public amenities are paid for by private development (today, the idea of publicly financed public amenities seems like a relic from the past). Surely the scale of any new development on one hundred acres (half of the total; the other half was for the highway) of new land to be created by Westway would have been huge, especially to fund the promised parks. But as Jane Jacobs asked in an interview with me in 1978, "If [Westway] is so great as a development, why don't they do it without the highway?" She answered her own question: "Because it is just meant to sell the highway."[3]

Proponents argued that the highway was needed to revitalize the heavily blighted Lower West Side. In fact, as soon as Westway was defeated, all sorts of nefarious investors in Lower West Side bars and strip joints closed up shop, sold their properties, and paved the way for the genuine rebirth along the inland side of the roadway. Those investors had expected to cash in big time when their property was taken by eminent domain for the expanded highway. Instead, the existing West Side Highway was upgraded, straightened, and even widened in some sections along its existing bed. Now, admirable loft conversions and new residential buildings, increasingly larger in scale, make it hard to believe anyone thought an expanded highway was needed to spark this area's rebirth. Instead, the shadow of the highway needed to be lifted to allow positive organic rebirth to occur.

A mostly state-financed Hudson River Park—the largest new park in the city since the creation of Central Park—emerged out of the defeat of Westway, primarily along the river side of the road, reflecting planning and design input from the three different neighborhoods that border it. This park put the lie to two oft-repeated beliefs: nothing big could get done anymore in the city, and Westway was needed to get a park. Even the *New York Times*, long an ardent advocate for Westway, noted that "this modest park is as big an urban planning success story as anything that has taken place in New York City in 100 years."[4] John Oakes sums it up well in a 1978 *New York Times* op-ed:

> The decline of New York's essentially efficient, energy-saving, decrepit transport system has reflected the decline of the city. But the massive rehabilitation of this arterial lifeline through a trade-in of Westway funds would be the most significant present step this city would take to assert its inner vitality and to underpin its future growth and development for the benefit of the masses of people who live and work here.

With the end of Westway, the turnaround in the city and region's transit system officially began. No mayor could have had as much of an impact on the city as the 1985 Westway defeat. If it had gone ahead, the highway would have cost end-less billions of state and local dollars beyond the most generous estimates—especially when federal funds ran out—and would have stunted the rebirth of the city that is so universally admired today. By comparison, Boston's Big Dig (which expanded a highway underground) was happening at the same time and was already years behind schedule, with a $15 billion price tag and growing from its original estimate of $2.75 billion.

It is hard to remember how difficult it was to get anywhere on the subway back then. Breakdowns, stalled trains, doors that didn't close, graffiti, and repellent garbage smells all made traversing the city difficult. Brooklyn neighborhoods were poorly served and, in some cases, almost inaccessible before the transit upgrade. Much of the progress has since been squandered, but those upgrades were a great example of the transformation of the city that transit rebuilding brought.

In 1956, the year of the Federal Aid Highway Act that began the building of the interstate system, New York instituted a policy of "deferred maintenance." As Robert Caro points out, "So superbly engineered and maintained had the system been previously . . . that it took years for this systematic neglect to take its toll."[5] By the late 1960s, it had almost reached bottom. "When Robert Moses came to power in 1934," Caro adds, "the city's mass transportation system was probably the best in the world. When he left power in 1968, it was quite possibly the worst."[6]

In 1985, Governor Hugh Carey and Mayor Ed Koch conceded defeat of Westway before the final congressional deadline to exchange committed highway funding for transit. In the Federal Aid Highway Act, there was a provision allowing localities to make this trade. Portland, Oregon, was the first to do it. Now, federal funding for the interstate highway program, of which Westway was a piece, was running out. In fact, there would never have been enough federal funding to complete Westway anyway. The highway funds designated for Westway went to fix the crumbling subways, buy new subway cars, and replace aging track and signals.[7] This was of enormous consequence for the city. Those federal transit funds were leveraged by the skillful head of the state Metropolitan Transportation Authority, Richard Ravitch, to raise significant additional state money to begin the much-needed rebuilding of the city's and region's transit system that had been financially starved since Robert Moses had shifted public transit funding to car-based transport.

Marcy Benstock reminds us as well that a majority in the US House of Representatives opposed funding Westway, identifying it as an unnecessary effort to create a real estate opportunity. "Editorials opposing it had run in newspapers across the country," Benstock noted, "and a rider was added to a highway bill to deny funding for Westway." She has long argued that "Westway was a plan to use federal highway funds and other public funds to create a site for real estate development using landfill and pile-supported platforms in the near shore waters of the Hudson River itself—in the environmentally critical habitat in the lower Hudson."

"The $1.3 billion in trade-in funds was a pittance in terms of need," noted Butzel, "but it came at a critical time at the beginning of the refocusing on transit that that controversy stimulated."[8]

It would be a mistake, however, to evaluate the Westway defeat only on the basis of the enormous transit benefit from the trade-in funds.[9] The positive ripple effects are equally significant. The Westway corridor was transformed on both sides of the roadway. Tribeca evolved into the richest zip code in the city. The loft-conversion trend had spread south into the neighborhood as SoHo lofts increased in price. It took a while

The historic Jane Street Hotel, built in 1907 to accommodate merchant seamen, was in the path of the proposed Westway. Now a boutique hotel, the modestly embellished brick-and-stone building is a designated landmark.

CREDIT: NEW YORK CITY LANDMARKS PRESERVATION COMMISSION

for amenities, like markets and schools, to follow, but follow they did. Amenities rarely show up before the vanguard population is in place.

Other neighborhoods around the city experienced tremendous infusions of new residents, lured in part by vastly improved transit service. A homeowner in now-popular Park Slope, Brooklyn, noted, "The trade-in made all the difference in my life. Before that, you could never count on getting back and forth to Manhattan to make a business meeting on time. You never knew whether your kid's lateness from school was something to worry about, and you wound up spending a fortune on cabs at night—if you could get them to take you across the bridge—because you never wanted to trust the subway after dark. I'd say the subway improvements maybe doubled the value of my house."

In addition, a new interest in the full 575 miles of New York City waterfront emerged after the intense focus on this five-mile stretch. Awareness of the Brooklyn waterfront intensified. The regional transit network shared in the investments, improving access to the city for local users, commuters, and visitors.

## THE CHOICE: HIGHWAYS OR CITIES

Until the mid-1980s, the idea that more and bigger highways solved traffic problems still prevailed. Increasing access by cars, both in cities and to suburbs, was the national focus after World War II. Few observers recognized that highways through cities and increased vehicular traffic in cities were inimical to urban life. Similarly, few experts understood fully how public transit was crucial to the functioning of a vibrant city. Word choice reflects beliefs. Officials talk about "investing" in highways but "subsidizing" transit. Federal funding for roads and airports is infinitely more generous than for transit, and the DC lobby for transit pales next to the lobbies for highways and airplanes.

The overwhelming predominance of highway provisions in transportation legislation is accepted as the norm. Some transportation legislation only mentions highways and makes little or no attempt to fund transit. The central concept of mobility is lost. The key question should be: Mobility for what?

Highways are designed to move vehicles; transit is designed to move people. The difference is like night and day. To really talk about the mobility of people and goods, public transit should be paramount.

Unquestionably, New York City today is much more accommodating of cars than during the Westway battle in the 1970s, when the City Planning Commission was forced to clamp down on the number of parking spaces in Midtown. A Friends of the Earth air-pollution lawsuit in 1977 put a restriction on the number of new parking spaces, but the restrictions expired and garages have not stopped proliferating since.

Additionally, some of the transportation ideas of the 1980s, before Westway was killed, still dominate. Some of today's conventional wisdom is even worse. Nevertheless, one should not ignore the differences. In New York City at least, public transit is valued more now than before the Westway fight. The country, however, still remains hopelessly imprisoned by car culture.

At its simplest, Westway was just another piece of the interstate highway system, stretching from 42nd Street down to the island's tip. The complexities are not visible at first. No one asked, for example, what would happen north of 42nd if Westway had been built. Another segment would have of course had to follow, right through Riverside Park, to accommodate the resulting bottleneck. But Westway looked clean and simple when it was presented. No neighborhoods would have been bisected or erased, although plenty would have suffered from the increased traffic of an expanded highway. No land would have been taken away. In fact, land would have been added with landfill, and the highway would have partially gone under it, through a tunnel. Deceptively, however, the Westway route was drawn as a straight line on all maps. The highly land-consumptive on- and off-ramps were not indicated, except for two ramps at the beginning and end of the road. None was shown between—which would have terrified neighborhoods. The additional ramps would have been revealed once the road was approved. And, of course, Westway was labeled as six lanes, hoping no one would notice that the existing inland highway would have been converted to a six-lane service road, making the total number of traffic lanes twelve. New highway proposals across the country often looked that simple. They still do.

Proponents of Westway manipulated these basic issues in the following ways:

- There was no public debate about whether to build a highway. Rather, the conversation was about which of five highway plans to adopt. Highway alternatives, not transportation alternatives, were offered. There was no option for "none of the above," even though the environmental impact review process required a no-road alternative. It was only about cars, not about transportation.
- Proponents danced around the issue of pollution. The 1970 Clean Air Act and its additions in 1973 created a built-in contradiction in proponents' arguments. If they argued that the estimated $4 billion roadway ($10,000 an inch) was necessary to relieve the anticipated increase in vehicular traffic (they argued at one point that traffic

would increase 8 percent), then the accompanying air pollution ran afoul of the Clean Air Act. If they minimized the potential traffic increase, then why spend all that money? When the opposition raised the air pollution issue, proponents switched to the economic value of the promised new housing, parks, and commercial development on half of the two hundred acres of landfill. Hearings were always segregated accordingly—pollution, improved traffic, or economic development—and the issues were never considered together, lest the internal contradictions reveal themselves.

- Even the idea of one hundred acres of new parkland was deceptively presented. There was no money to actually create any parks. In fact, the city couldn't even maintain the parks it had, most of which were in terrible shape. The parks would, of course, inevitably have to be paid for by the developers of what would surely be enormous towers.

In addition to the above controversies, opponents knew they were fighting for the crucial habitat of the striped bass, who spent their winter amid the West Side piers before heading upriver to spawn. Mitch Bernard, the NRDC lawyer, had worked on the Westway suit. He pointed out in an interview, "It was fundamentally about the interaction of the natural and built environment and the harmony between them. But it was also about protecting the striped bass, enforcing the Clean Water Act, and respecting scientific fact and the rule of law over economic and political power. The argument was never about the roadway per se." He added, "The *New York Times* called opponents obstructionists, but in fact the law prohibited building this road. Proponents lied and got the original permit by covering up the impact on the striped bass. This was caught during litigation. The fight was between truth and the law over economic development and political power."

Marcy Benstock explained, "The litigation was also important, because Mitch Bernard established great case law under the Clean Water Act, helping future efforts across the country." Benstock also pointed out that, although not widely reported, "the US EPA, the US Interior Department's Fish and Wildlife Service, and the US Commerce Department's National Marine Fisheries Service were among the powerful and well-resourced public agencies that opposed the Army Corps' Clean Water Act permit for Westway for seven years, and career civil servants and administrators at those agencies courageously put their careers on the line to save that habitat and the law."

The final issue on which the permit was denied was the bait and switch with the facts tried by the feds. "Their earliest Corps of Engineers studies said Westway would have a significant adverse impact on the Hudson River striped bass," Bernard explained. But then the Clean Water Act was passed, which would have prohibited the Army Corps of Engineers from granting a permit for something that created a significant adverse impact. Nevertheless, in the final environmental documents, with no new data or credible analysis, the corps said the highway would not have such a significant adverse impact. "Judge Griesa called that conclusion a 'sheer fiction,'" Bernard added. "The court ruled after a seven-week trial that the corps' finding was arbitrary and contrary to the facts in the record."

At that point, the fight was over. Not much time was left for New York to trade in its committed highway funds, so on September 30, 1985, the governor and mayor threw in the towel and the Westway proposal died. It was one of the Fund's most significant victories.

## THE THEATERS

In the early 1970s, Times Square was still the beating heart of a struggling city. The unique area was not yet overrun by chain stores and a shopping-mall atmosphere. It was the country's ultimate theater district: the Broadway George M. Cohan gave his regards to and the neon strip Las Vegas imitated. It remained the place where the New Year began for the nation when the ball dropped from atop the former Times Tower. It was the symbol of a city that relished its image as the cultural mecca of the nation.

The Theater District had always been a predominantly low-scale area of small interests and large surprises, where the new stood cheek by jowl with the old, and where legitimate businesses operated next door to disreputable ones. A special mixed-use character still accompanied the theaters and restaurants. The Theater District was one of the last Manhattan neighborhoods not yet experiencing the new momentum evident on Park and Sixth Avenues. When city officials labeled the area underdeveloped in the early 1980s, they meant that the city was willing to make generous concessions to developers building large towers there. The area became the new frontier for development. For the first time, it needed protection.

Twenty-one legitimate theaters had been demolished since the 1940s.[10] Theaters had become an endangered species. Whole block fronts were being assembled for development. Purposeful blight was evident along the West Side Highway corridor and around Times Square. "Deliberate neglect, as a number of unscrupulous developers have discovered over the years," writes Tony Hiss in a 1987 *New Yorker* article, "has a powerful perceptual effect: dirty, broken, or boarded-up windows, peeling paint, and a sagging cornice are painful to look at; consider the word 'eyesore.'" This is sometimes called "planners' blight": when an official plan is created for an area, new investment stops, maintenance slips, people move out, and buildings deteriorate.[11] Under these circumstances, the district never had a chance to regenerate naturally, as impending city plans kept owners waiting to cash in. While they waited, their property continued to decay.

Real estate and political leaders promoted the misguided notion that only large-scale new building plans could bring significant renewal. In New York, economic health has been erroneously measured by the level of new construction. Few challenged the validity of that idea at the time, and many still don't. Atlanta architect John Portman's formula for hotels was the flavor of the moment nationwide. Portman's Times Square hotel design—fortresslike, focused exclusively inward on its huge atrium, hostile to the street—was as anti-city a design as possible.

The battle over the theater demolition and new replacement hotel evolved into a metaphor for clashing values and competing visions. The powers behind it were singularly focused: new development at all cost. They were an influential collection of power brokers, city and state officials, construction unions, theater owners, and real estate spokesmen. On the other side were actors, playwrights, artists, preservationists, and culture defenders. It was an uneven battle that made the support of Joan and the Fund all the more courageous and critical.

In the late 1960s, long before this battle, New York had initiated incentive zoning—a tool that later gained popularity throughout the country. Simply, builders gained extra rentable floor space in exchange for providing amenities that might otherwise be too expensive to be in the builder's own interest. In 1967, a special theater district was created to encourage—through such bonuses—development that would save Broadway from decay and loss of theaters.[12] A developer was given extra bulk if he included a new theater. There was also a provision, which seems actually quaint today, requiring that for each new commercial theater, a nonprofit theater must be built as well. This was a real innovation and led to the construction of the Circle in the Square and the American Place Theatre, both nonprofits triggered by the building of the Minskoff and Uris (renamed the Gershwin) Theatres. No bonus was given for saving and restoring an existing theater or, for that matter, saving any worthy existing structure.

Meanwhile, the great old Broadway theaters languished. Approximately one hundred theaters were built between 1895 and 1929 with incomparable workmanship and materials, such as horsehair insulation and jaw-dropping plaster work.[13] By the early 1970s, half of these theaters had been either torn down or converted into pornographic-movie houses. American theater was at a low point, a perfect storm for wrongheaded proposals.

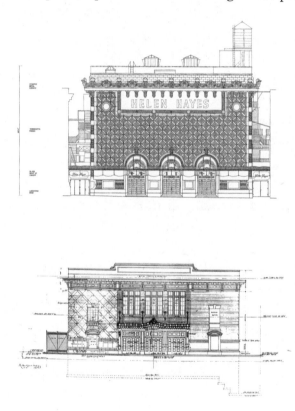

The 1917 Morosco Theatre (T), designed by Herbert J. Knapp and known for its incomparable acoustics, and the 1911 Moorish revival Helen Hayes (B), designed by Herts and Tallant, were demolished in 1982 to make way for the fifty-story Marriot Marquis hotel, designed by John Portman. CREDIT: HISTORIC AMERICAN BUILDINGS SURVEY (LIBRARY OF CONGRESS)

Broadway had increasingly become dominated by three theater-owning chains: Nederlander, Shubert, and Jujamcyn. The Morosco and Helen Hayes were independently owned and, because of their high quality and desirability, provided stiff competition to the dominant chains, which made them vulnerable. The false notion that removing buildings fixes social and physical problems was thoroughly entrenched in the city, and every new building proposal was greeted with accolades. So it was that architect John Portman and Mayor John Lindsay announced the Times Square hotel project in 1973. Three theaters—the Morosco, Helen Hayes, and Bijou—would be demolished, all on theater-packed 45th Street.[14]

In fact, 45th Street also had a thriving hotel, nine mostly small theaters (some converted to other uses), a movie house, restaurants, and other small enterprises. Actor Bernard Hughes, writing on the op-ed page of the *New York Times* on February 10, 1980, describes the block as "the quintessential Broadway Street, a concentrate of what the theater has to offer with musicals, comedy and straight drama thriving in proximity." Nevertheless, officials immediately set about expediting the permit that would demolish all of this. A zoning change permitted the new hotel to include both a movie house and a new theater, seven floors of shopping, six floors of convention space, and a street-level café. It was to be financed completely privately.

In less than one month, the project was approved, an extremely speedy turnaround in a city where developers usually complain of a tedious, expensive, and often delayed process. Nevertheless, Portman failed to get financing, and by mid-December the project was dead.

Many cities and architecture critics were smitten by Portman's style, which felt refreshingly new at the time. Portman's Peachtree Plaza in Atlanta, with its huge atrium and glass elevator built in the 1960s, was highly influential, but not every city fell under the architect's spell. Boston rejected a design by him for the waterfront the same year New York welcomed him. "Portman is selling an architectural package that can be dropped on any city which gives encouragement," wrote *Boston Globe* columnist Ian Menzies on March 22, 1973.

In 1978, DC resoundingly rejected a plan of his that included tearing down the 1835 National Theater, the oldest continuously operating legitimate theater in the country. Instead, a different project was accepted: a smaller complex of offices, hotel, and stores surrounding the historic theater, along with the theater's refurbishment.

In 1978, Mayor Ed Koch took office and quickly sought out Portman to renew his interest in building the fifty-story hotel. Although proposals had been floated to give developers the same bonus to preserve and renovate a historic theater as was available to build a new one, the idea went nowhere. Meanwhile, historic theaters all over the country were being restored as centerpieces of downtown rebirth. Ada Louise Huxtable—who actually gave Portman's style a positive review, praising the hotel's design as "peculiarly appropriate to its site"—wrote that there were old theaters "restored and adapted for modern cultural uses and serving as economic catalysts for the re-awakening of downtown."[15] In fact, by 1978 some of the biggest developers in the country had caught on to the economic wisdom of recycling the solid remnants of

In 1982, John Portman's Marriot Marquis hotel replaced a whole block that included the Helen Hayes and Morosco Theatres, the smaller Gaiety, Bijou, and Astor Theaters, and the Hotel Piccadilly. CREDIT: (c) 1973 R. GARDNER, IMAGE COURTESY THE PORTMAN ARCHIVES

the past.[16] Portman's design formula left no room for imaginative blending of old and new buildings. The 1976 tax law changes even gave developers advantages for preserving historic buildings. But instead, NYC officials sweetened the pot for Portman with local, state, and federal subsidies for new construction that eventually totaled more than $100 million. The design was also changed to remove some of the originally promised amenities.

Activists, primarily led by local community board member Barbara Handman, tried to interest the city and Portman in siting the hotel on the east side of Broadway between 48th and 49th Streets, replacing assorted pornographic businesses. This "would have done twenty different good things at once to improve the area, and not one bad thing," Handman said. "Portman wouldn't consider it, even though it was the same size lot."

The professional theater community valued the theaters as spaces for art, not real estate, and considered the Morosco and Helen Hayes to be of superior, irreplaceable quality. Recently built theaters convinced the professionals that any replacement would never remotely live up to the historic standard. The acoustics and other details could never be replicated. In April 1978, a staff member from the city's Landmarks Preservation Commission told me off the record, "Architecturally, the Helen Hayes is one of the finest theaters in the Times Square area." The commission ignored that staff judgment and refused to designate it a landmark, the first step in a long line of city and state failures. Disingenuously, officials tried to argue that the Morosco (1,009 seats) and Helen Hayes (1,160 seats including the second balcony) were too small to be economically viable. (A *New York Times* editorial from January 20, 1982, refers to them inappropriately as "two unused and probably unusable theaters.") The new 1,500 seat Portman theater would be more appropriate, proponents argued.

The entire Portman design was disastrous. Sydney Schanberg wrote in the *New York Times* on March 13, 1982: "Everybody's always trying to stand in the way of progress. Take the plan to put up the Portman Hotel—a modernist concrete bunker worthy of 'The Guns of Navarone.'" Today, thankfully, the hotel is mostly hidden behind a huge, well-lit sign.

Architect and critic Michael Sorkin wrote a scathing critique of the hotel plan in the *Wall Street Journal* in January 1982. "Mr. Portman's buildings are like giant spaceships, offering close encounters with the city, but not too close. The buildings are always adamant about their alien status."

Both Joan and I independently heard about what was unfolding from the same source. Playwright John Guare and his wife, preservationist and former head of the American Academy in Rome Adele Chatfield-Taylor, beseeched us separately to do something to save the theaters, particularly the Helen Hayes, which was the more architecturally notable of the two.[17] On November 19, 1979, I published an article for *New York Magazine* entitled "Save the Helen Hayes," the first appearance in the press of a critical view of the project.

Joan, meanwhile, "appealed to the usual colleagues," she recalled. "I went to the board of the Municipal Art Society, to Ada Louise Huxtable, to [*New York Times* architecture writer] Paul Goldberger. It seemed so obviously the wrong thing to do. It threw me for a loop that no one seemed interested. Was no one willing to lift a finger to challenge Shubert and Nederlander? In fact, they promoted the proposed new development. They didn't own the Helen Hayes and Morosco. If they had, things might have been different. The Fund got involved in trying to rally people." This was one of Joan and the Fund's most activist causes. But neither she nor the Fund's prestige, nor that of the scores of marquee stars and civic leaders, meant anything in the end.

Portman, however, wasn't having an easy time securing either private financing or the potential federal funding. At any moment, the city or state urban development corporation (UDC) shepherding the project could have jumped in. They certainly were hearing the well-articulated protests from the Broadway and national theater communities and local and national preservationists. Opponents were mobilizing and speaking out, although the press mostly ignored their efforts.

A Save the Theaters committee was organized in 1979 by Actors' Equity under the leadership of actors Lenore Loveman and Sandy Lundwall. Preservationist Jack Goldstein, who had recently moved to NYC from DC, joined them to help. They had begun a long series of protest activities, including testifying at public hearings. I remember Sandy Lundwall saying to me, "I don't know how any of these things work, the Planning Commission or any of these agencies." I replied: "You will know more than a graduate planning student by the time this is over."

Also in 1979, Joan helped organize a group called Save Our Broadway (SOB) to formalize the efforts of the few preservationists and community activists willing to take this fight to court. In a short time, SOB merged with Save the Theaters. Petitions were circulated, gathering more than two hundred thousand signatures. Ads were taken out in the *New York Times*. Rallies were held, the first one in February 1980.

Film and stage stars met privately with key players, including Mayor Koch and John Portman. The list of supporters read like a who's who of stage and screen, including President Ronald Reagan's close friends Charlton Heston and James Stewart. At every turn, public officials accused these artists of sentimentalism and emotionalism, which had nothing to do with the real world of "economic development" and "progress." The press carried the same tune. The Portman project, the papers claimed, was the "rescue," "linchpin," "centerpiece," or "key" to the revitalization of the "decaying and crime-ridden," "ramshackle," or "deteriorating," Times Square area. The irreplaceable qualities of the theaters were ignored, as if they were not the real value of the district.

Clearly, the Landmarks Preservation Commission was not inclined to designate; the mayor was a big booster of the new hotel at all costs. Instead, the commission designated the remaining twenty-three historic theaters. But even that was unacceptable to the theater owners calling the shots. They sued to stop the designations. A lawsuit had been inevitable, and Joan turned to John Adams, head of the Natural Resources Defense Council. NRDC had been organized in 1970 to be, in effect, the law firm for the environmental movement, starting with Storm King, the proposed hydroelectric power plant on the Hudson River just below Newburgh (see Chapter 6). Joan had been an active NRDC board member and steady financial supporter from the organization's beginning. NRDC's Mitch Bernard successfully defended the theaters' designations.

Until now, the environment had been defined primarily as the natural environment, and the focus of NRDC and other environmental organizations was entirely on nature. But Joan trusted Adams's understanding and values. "We needed his help," recalled Joan. "John agreed immediately, but he had to go to the board. It was a hard sell." Some board members strongly resisted this major policy change, "but somehow he got the board to agree." This was a significant moment. Environmental issues would never again be limited to the natural; the built and the natural were seen as symbiotic and forever joined.

John Adams and his wife, Patricia, live in a classic old farmhouse deep in the environmentally rich Beaverkill Valley on the west side of the Hudson, about two hours from the city. The valley is an area of dense forest, farms, and fly-fishing along Beaverkill River in the Catskill Mountains.

Interviewed in his home, Adams recalled: "Some board members had to swallow hard. We were already moving strongly in some directions and we were shaking up some people. But I want to make clear that this issue wasn't difficult. It really wasn't. It was a question of if we were too small. We had a tiny staff looking at issues in every aspect of the world—nuclear energy, Russian arms, early climate change. So it was not the issue that was the problem, and we have a huge urban program now."[18]

Joan had introduced Mitch Bernard to John Adams after funding his work litigating for the rights of the homeless for the Coalition for the Homeless (see Chapter 7) and then its spin-off, the Association to Benefit Children. "There is no way NRDC would have been involved in the theater fight if Joan had not funded me to come do this work." Bernard said. "You could in a court of law try to hold off forces who think they are the custodians of the cultural heritage when they were just real estate developers dressed up as theater owners. Imagine if more theaters had succumbed to the wrecking ball?" The lawsuit to save the theaters lost. As Bernard noted, "The courts usually defer to the local authority on land use issues, no matter how big the army of opposing citizens."

Joan also appealed to her good friend, Public Theater producer Joe Papp, who was engrossed in his own theater downtown. Joan had been an early supporter and board member of the Public Theater. On the street with a microphone or in a hotel room on the phone, whenever Papp got involved, he was a tireless demon. He joined the cause as an energetic ally, but entreaties to local and state officials were still being ignored.

However, Papp was going to make sure that if the issue lost, the world would know what was going down. He effectively orchestrated the drama's final scene in March 1982, with three weeks of protest in front of the Morosco, including three days of around-the-clock marathon readings of plays that had been presented at the two theaters, including Jason Robards' recitation from Eugene O'Neill's *Long Day's Journey into Night*, in which he had starred at the Helen Hayes. The audience was hushed; it was "one of street theater's finest hours," noted *New York Times* reporter John Corry. But only the final scene of this American tragedy played out on the public stage. The *New York Times* waited until the day after demolition to extol the architectural splendor of the Helen Hayes Theatre. As in similar tales in too many cities, the real action had already played out offstage. The protestors, including me, had poured onto

45th Street over several days, as a parade of actors read from an assortment of plays. Finally, on the night before demolition of the Morosco was to begin, hundreds of us were hauled off in paddy wagons to be booked and then released.[19]

## A HUGE LOSS TO THE CITY

The sad truth is that the city could have had it all. At one point, a state urban development corporation executive confessed privately to Save the Theaters leader Lenore Loveman that an alternative design—as legally required by the environmental impact statement—had never been explored.[20] The UDC official sketched crudely how the hotel could be built over the theaters, suggesting that if an architect explored that possibility, UDC would have to consider it. Barbara Handman approached fellow community board member and award-winning architect Lee Harris Pomeroy. Pomeroy developed a plan meant only to show feasibility.[21] It eliminated the proposed new 1,500-seat theater, saved the two existing ones, and retained all other Portman features. Pomeroy was taken no more seriously than the entire four years of thoughtful opposition.

Clearly, the bulldoze-and-replace Robert Moses approach that marked the 1950s was alive and well. It continues today. In this game, the government's role is to nourish the big project with tax incentives, zoning bonuses, and funding subsidies in the name of encouraging development and getting things done. New York's highly subsidized real estate market is never recognized as subsidized, just as "the market." But there is no real market; there are deals with different types of public support. Today, every project is a public-private partnership—a private project with public financial and/or zoning support.

A new zoning principle established at the time of the theater controversy plays out in a bigger way today. Unused air rights above a historic theater could be transferred anywhere within the special theater zoning district, which was created in 1982 by the City Planning Commission. The boundaries went from 42nd Street to 59th Street between Eighth and Sixth Avenues. Recently, this kind of "long distance" air-rights transfer has been playing out in Midtown East, with new super-tall towers rising as a result.[22]

Until the theater fight, air-rights transfers were provided only to landmarks, as compensation for preserving something of architectural, cultural, and public value that would be lost if the building owner sought to redevelop. The landmark owner was afforded something non-landmark buildings did not get because of the landmark's value as a public asset. This was a fundamental way to offer public appreciation for a decidedly public benefit.

In the 1982 special theater zoning district, the transfer of a landmark's air rights was strictly limited to "abutting areas or across the street."[23] This landmark air-rights benefit created and maintained the distinction between a public asset and private wealth. Some landmarks were locked in between sites that could not accommodate an air-rights transfer—because the adjacent sites were already built to the maximum the zoning allowed—and, thus, were just out of luck. But, in 1998, another zoning amendment allowed for the expansion of the transfer of development rights—not just to adjacent sites but to anywhere in the theater zoning district. No parallel compensation had existed for a non-landmark property, and for good reason; non-landmark buildings were adequately covered by zoning laws and had the freedom to alter their site in ways that landmarks couldn't. But since that transfer expansion, air rights have been floated around the Theater District for new buildings and eventually led to the principle that air rights should be floatable in special zoning districts in other parts of town. This is what is now happening in Midtown East.

The timeless and fundamental principle had been that one bought real estate based on the value of the building, not for the air rights above it that could be sold in the future. This has become less and less true.

This is a far-reaching consequence. Over the years since, the transfer of air rights has gotten so out of control elsewhere in the city that suddenly a pier in the Hudson River can transfer air rights to an inland site blocks away, across the West Side Highway, to make possible a behemoth development inappropriately towering over the low-scaled Greenwich Village neighborhood. There are no limits anymore, nor do there seem to be limits on irrationality. The distinction between density and congestion is lost. Everything is measured by its potential for large-scale private gain. This is a sad state.

The theater saga demonstrates better than any other how things really work and why a vigilant, activist public—nourished and sometimes led by an activist foundation—is so vital to speaking truth to power and taking on battles that are only sometimes won. The struggle over Westway reflected similar forces at play as in the theater fight, but the power brokers were different and the Westway battle ended in victory. In both stories, Joan is an example of how a visionary funder can help create or support resistance to harmful ideas and powerful forces only out for their own economic gain. Both game-changing cases demonstrate that the days of looking at the environment as a discrete set of issues are gone. They show how everything in a city is linked—economics, politics, historic preservation, and environmental justice—in what Jane Jacobs called an urban ecology. Joan saw early on how all this fit, woven into the fabric of city life. Both cases demonstrate the intractability of city and real estate leaders, making Joan's principled and expensive efforts all the more meaningful.

While the Westway and Save the Theaters fights may have been the biggest battles, they were not the only ones Joan was willing to support. Sometimes Fund support went to a critical study or pamphlet to publicize a challenge. Sometimes it went to an advocacy effort. Many times, support went to a lawsuit, unusual among foundations.

In 1986, the Upper East Side neighborhood group CIVITAS discovered that a developer was building a thirty-one-story apartment tower that was twelve stories higher than the city's zoning law allowed. That set off a five-year fight, including a lawsuit financed by the Fund, which resulted in a far-reaching settlement that involved the negotiating skills of then mayor David Dinkins. The developer was forced to remove twelve stories to complete the building. This was an extraordinary community-led victory.

As David Dunlap writes in the *New York Times*, "Neither the builders nor opponents of the project could recall so drastic a penalty for a zoning violation, which the developers have consistently attributed to an error in a city map. By the same token, there seem to have been few violations on such an obvious and large scale anywhere in the nation."[24]

All around the city over the years, fights ensued to save landmark-quality buildings that had or had not yet been officially designated. Sometimes litigation ensued. Sometimes just aggressive and expensive advocacy was involved. The J.M. Kaplan Fund—and equally often the Vincent Astor Foundation—supported these efforts. When the landmark McKim, Mead & White–designed Metropolitan Club on Fifth Avenue and 60th Street proposed in 1987 to sell its air rights for an adjacent tower, requiring one column to go through the building, the Friends of the Upper East Side went to the Fund to pay for a study to show the inappropriateness of the proposal. The Pierre hotel, Harmonie Club, Municipal Art Society, and preservationists all over town joined the opposition that led to a denial of the proposal presented by the Landmarks Preservation Commission.

Similarly, when the New-York Historical Society on Central Park West proposed building a twenty-three-story Hugh Hardy tower over and behind the York & Sawyer–designed original building, the Fund supported the Landmark West! group and citywide effort to stop it, successfully.

The Grace Church at Broadway and 10th Street wanted to tear down its adjacent houses that matched the church's Gothic facade to build a new gym for its highly regarded Grace Church School.[25] The houses are an incomparable part of the 1834 church site, designed by James Renwick. Instead, a

$10,000 Fund grant demonstrated how the new gym could be built behind the historic facades. It was, and the houses remain intact on the outside.

Columbia University preservation students, led by their professor, architect Robert A.M. Stern, and the head of Columbia's preservation program, James Marston Fitch, waged the fight on the Upper West Side to save the stately, red-brick Association Home, designed by Richard Morris Hunt, at 103rd and Amsterdam Avenue.[26] Robert Moses wanted to tear it down as part of his urban renewal plan that replaced a large swath of the Upper West Side. Eventually, the city bought the building and designated it a landmark in 1983. It sat empty until, with great community support, the American Youth Hostels bought and restored it as a 670-bed hostel—the largest in North America—opening in 1990, with a $250,000 grant from the Fund to restore the garden.

The Fund stepped in as the first philanthropic funder, with the Vincent Astor Foundation, in another big case that took on citywide significance. In 1986, Donald Trump sought to build Television City on the far West Side, from 59th to 72nd Streets at the river over the rail yards. His mammoth proposal included 18.5 million square feet built on a platform at the level of the elevated West Side Highway, like a huge wall blocking visibility and access to the river. On top would be the tallest building in the world, flanked by six extra-tall residential towers. Underneath would be the largest regional shopping mall east of the Mississippi and parking for 7,400 cars. Fortunately, it was so outrageous—a threat to retail all over the city and potentially drawing enough traffic to choke the whole island of

Donald Trump proposed building a six-story shopping mall and garage from 59th to 72nd Street, with a 150-story tower on top and flanked by six other towers set in a park, walling off the entire Upper West Side from the river.
CREDIT: BETTMANN / GETTY IMAGES

Manhattan—that garnering citywide opposition was not difficult, but rallying West Siders, fundraising in living rooms, and circulating flyers was still not enough.

This is another enormously significant David and Goliath story. A book about this citizen-led battle has been written by architect Steve Robinson, a West Sider at the time and a member of the small group that started the nonprofit Westpride to oppose Trump's plan.[27] Eventually, with a six-thousand-member organization (including some headline names), a lawsuit, and considerable direct negotiations with Trump himself, the activists beat the proposal and secured a mediocre but infinitely better alternative, with no shopping mall or oversized parking garage. The project was built over several years and by different owners, and includes a unique waterfront park with total design input from the community and citywide civic organizations. Over four years, the Fund donated $115,000 and the Vincent Astor Foundation $95,000.

If a battle over a landmark, or even just a bad new development plan, emerged in some neighborhood, and a grassroots group arose to fight it, Joan was there to support the local voice firmly—even if it meant an expensive lawsuit—believing that "every community should have the opportunity to have their opinions heard."

# 6

# A GREEN THUMB

In 1965, Whitney North Seymour Jr., a former US attorney for the Southern District of New York and a vigorous advocate for city parks and historic preservation, approached J.M. Kaplan with a modest request. The Park Association, of which he was head, had been advocating for some time for the creation of small neighborhood parks and play areas, converted from vacant lots that were often filled with garbage.[1] Most of them were situated in the middle of blocks in poor neighborhoods, a great distance from the city's large, well-known parks.

Seymour's request was for a grant to establish three tiny parks of approximately two thousand square feet, each on a vacant, city-owned lot to demonstrate the value of small neighborhood parks. Each park would have a community sponsor—a local connection with whom park users could identify. At the time, the city standard for a park was three acres or more fronting on an avenue. What Seymour and the Park Association had in mind was tiny in comparison, and midblock. J.M. Kaplan responded enthusiastically, and the city's first vest-pocket park, designed by Columbia University architecture students, was created at 65 East 128th Street, between

The vest-pocket park on East 128th Street, funded by the J.M. Kaplan Fund, was one of three created in 1965 that redefined the concept of a park.
CREDIT: CATRYNA TEN EYCK SEYMOUR

Fifth and Lenox Avenues. Two more quickly followed on the same block, which now had a "tot lot," "teen lot," and "adult sitting area." Murals embellished the walls of adjacent buildings. Low-income neighbors were thrilled by this addition to their playground-scarce neighborhood. "Robert Moses built 255 playgrounds in New York City during the 1930s," Caro points out. "He built one playground in Harlem, one in what became Bedford Stuyvesant."[2]

Douglas Feiden, writing in the *Wall Street Journal* on July 29, 2015, about the fiftieth anniversary of this innovation, notes: "The vest-pocket parks redefined the concept of parkland. By creating tiny greenswards where there had been gaps in the street bed, they brought the parks to the doorstep of people in congested park-starved areas."

It didn't take long for the concept to go national. Senators Robert F. Kennedy and Jacob Javits toured the site with US interior secretary Stewart Udall. Months later, mayoral candidate John Lindsay pledged to create dozens of these parks throughout the city. Soon, other cities followed. Over time, the simple concept morphed into urban farms and, in Latino neighborhoods, casitas that serve as vital community public spaces.[3]

Actually, Kaplan had supported an earlier playground and plaza that remains today, mid-block between the drab urban-renewal Stephen Wise Towers on 90th Street between Amsterdam and Columbus on the Upper West Side. There is a water feature, a fresco on one of the tower walls, and eighteen abstract cement play horses in the sand. "The Stephen Wise Plaza/Playground represented a new approach to creating urban space," notes James Trainor, who has written about the generation of park designers who were creating new sculptural forms for playscapes at the time.[4]

Joan assumes J.M. was approached to fund this by then NYC Housing Authority commissioner Ira Robbins, a progressive housing expert and friend of J.M.'s. "Those clever folks who knew how to strategically stroll along with JM on his long walk from his 12th Street office to his 80th Street house," Joan said with a laugh. "JM was a friend of Stephen Wise [after whom the towers are named]," Joan explained. Wise, a well-known rabbi and Zionist leader, died in 1949, but Joan remembered him visiting the family house when she was young.

An aggressive activist group, appropriately named the Green Guerillas—founded by Liz Christy in 1973, with Tessa Huxley as the first executive director—also soon emerged to bring green life to abandoned lots leftover from demolition and rebuilding projects. In the 1960s and '70s, these spaces, often filled with garbage, were a blatant sign of the city's deterioration. Not letting fences deter them, this small, determined group, supported by the Fund, started to throw seeds into empty lots, plant sunflowers on the medians of major streets, and hang flower boxes on the windowsills of abandoned buildings. The Green Guerillas were one of the thousands of small, grassroots efforts that started when the city had hit its lowest ebb. The group was a tiny indication of city life reemerging, like the lone daisy cropping up in the crack of a sidewalk.

With their small successes, the Green Guerillas' vision grew. They took on a large, debris-filled lot at the corner of Houston Street and the Bowery and, with neighborhood volunteers, created a community garden. Vegetable plants and seeds were donated by local stores and nurseries. Community gardens around the city rapidly became a way to reclaim abandoned lots, develop new resident connections, and create neighborhood groups to take on local problems in a concerted way. They all fed the renewal momentum.

The transformation of empty lots—mostly city owned—evolved into a movement that eventually clashed, in 1999, with a policy initiative of Mayor Rudolph Giuliani. The mayor wanted all city-owned lots sold through auctions for low-income housing development. The public uproar was tremendous; activists were baffled by the mayor acting as if no other options for such development existed. Even state attorney general Eliot Spitzer sued the city to prevent the auctions. The controversy lasted into the administration of Mayor Michael Bloomberg, first elected in 2002, when a compromise was struck. Actress Bette Midler started the New York Restoration Project (NYRP) in 1995 to revitalize neglected green spaces throughout the city, especially in low-income neighborhoods. Midler, along with the Trust for Public Land, stepped in to buy over one hundred lots in 2000. The J.M. Kaplan Fund contributed $1 million toward the Trust for Public Land acquisition, the largest single grant ever made by the Fund in NYC. In 2002, over three hundred additional gardens were placed under the jurisdiction of the city's Parks Department, and at least two hundred were ultimately made available for housing development. Midler's NYRP still owns fifty-two, and the trust had seventy but eventually turned ownership over to land trusts led by community gardeners.

Today, hundreds of community gardens and a full array of sponsoring nonprofit groups are found all over the city, growing food for local families, introducing children to farmwork, and creating gathering spots for the elderly to meet and sit. These community efforts often inspire action addressing other local needs. Just the creation of a garden can bring together people in the community for the first time. As Tony Wood noted, "Often they became meeting and training grounds where people, often immigrants, first got involved in their neighborhood and civic activism." The Fund has long been a supporter of the

Trust for Public Land and was an early supporter of the land-trust movement.

Former Fund staffer Suzanne Davis recalled that first and foremost the Fund was interested in people with great ideas who would galvanize efforts to bring positive change in the arts, civil rights and civil liberties, and the physical city. "A person would come to us with an idea," Davis said in an interview. "Sometimes we provided technical know-how to get it set up and we'd help refine the proposal. We didn't want to give money for a study if they'd already done the research. We'd say, 'Let's just do it.'"

Seated in her West Side living room, Davis—thin, dark haired, and highly animated—remembered her "favorite story, just exactly the kind of grant, illustrating what you want in people." Architect Barry Benepe had sent in a three-page letter, no letterhead, proposing to introduce farmers' markets in New York as a place where farmers could bring their goods from around the state and sell directly to the public." He was working with Robert Lewis, then chief marketing representative of the New York State Department of Agriculture and Markets. Their primary purpose was to preserve farmland around the state and protect it from excessive encroaching development. When farms were failing, farmers often gave up and sold the land to developers.

Davis immediately thought this was a good idea and, since he'd already done a lot of research, she said, "Barry you don't need money for study. Let's just open a market, a Green-market." So Davis put him in touch with the Council on the Environment, a nonprofit group, because he didn't have a tax exemption.[5] They immediately agreed to sponsor the project. They opened the first market on an empty lot on Second Avenue under the 59th Street bridge. That one was so successful, they had opened one at Union Square by the end of the year. "And, of course, the project fit perfectly with all Mr. Kaplan's interests in farming and farmland," Davis added.

The Greenmarket is another good example of the kind of innovative change at the grassroots, below the experts' radar, that stimulated the rebirth of the city, one neighborhood at a time. Experts have a difficult time recognizing each modest

The Greenmarket at Union Square, 14th Street, was one of the earliest and most successful in the city.

Credit: Museum of the City of New York / Getty Images

effort as a seed for larger, significant, and positive change. The Greenmarket led to an opening of Union Square as a public gathering place for all kinds of people—young and old—instead of just a hangout for intimidating drug dealers. Even more significantly, it spurred the revival of the neighborhood and beyond, as chic new restaurants opened to take advantage of the local, organic produce that was required for a new style of cooking. Residential loft conversions and stores followed, a classic pattern of locally initiated urban change that never gets the credit it deserves for genuinely renewing places of all kinds and sizes. This same phenomenon could be observed around the country: at the revived Pike Place Market in Seattle, rescued from urban-renewal demolition by a fierce local fight, at the revived Dane County Farmers' Market in Madison, Wisconsin, and everywhere in between. Markets have long had a community-building and small-business-spawning role. As of 2018, more than fifty Greenmarkets can be found around New York's five boroughs.

If you look beyond the standard measurements and expert prognoses, this is the kind of turnaround project you find in communities and cities of all sizes around the country and abroad. Recognition of significant early efforts is missed by those who wait for statistics and big moves to reflect change. But new movements and, surely, big winds of change *always* start small and local.

Planting trees, reclaiming vacant lots, establishing neighborhood gardens, cleaning shoreline spaces, and advocating for public park improvements were among the many ways New Yorkers, often with Fund support, were finding to rescue the city during its worst financial crisis.[6] A glance at the Fund's grant lists in the late 1970s reveals a telling story. Joining Green Guerillas in local gardening was the Horticultural Society of New York, which was planting gardens at local public libraries. The Street Tree Consortium was planting trees and caring for those that needed attention. The Staten Island Council on the Arts was saving the historic Grymes Hill area of Stapleton as open space for community use.

Well-known parks advocate the Parks Council was working to redesign and revive Bryant Park. Robert Moses, who gets a lot of credit for creating parks, had had Bryant Park reconstructed ("wrecked," as Joan described it) in the 1930s in such a forbidding manner that the park was attractive only to homeless people and drug dealers. Journalist William H. Whyte, famous for advocating pedestrian-friendly street designs, developed the strategy to revive Bryant Park into the worldwide symbol of park reclamation it is today.[7]

The impact of all these efforts on the city was cumulative, but sometimes small grants had their own large impact. Each of the Fund grants supporting these community gardens, parks, and nature improvements was modest at best and by no means the only support these groups received. But the individual efforts were having a noticeable effect on the city as the despairing '70s turned into the hopeful '80s.

## CENTRAL PARK BREAKS NEW GROUND

Nothing better epitomized the state of the city's fiscal, physical, and moral decay than the condition of Central Park, one of the symbols of New York City worldwide. It is also a good example of how New Yorkers of all income levels rallied to rescue the park and turn it into an example of the city's rebirth. The effort began during the administration of Mayor Abraham Beame and continued in a bigger way under Mayor Ed Koch.

In 1976, Elizabeth Barlow Rogers, a landscape designer, landscape preservationist, and writer, wrote an eye-opening article in *New York Magazine*, "32 Ways Your Time or Money Can Rescue Central Park," focusing attention on the legendary park's desperate condition.[8] The Parks Department budget was being slashed, as was the full city budget, because the city's fiscal crisis was at its worst point. Everything in the park was in a varying state of deterioration. Benches were broken or missing. Stone bridges were crumbling. Playground equipment was damaged beyond repair. Paths were disrupted. Bushes were overgrown. The park's extraordinary landmark buildings were in dire condition. Weeds had taken over lawns. Trees were dying. The article struck a nerve for people ready to do something. It was the same spirit behind the creation of block parties, neighborhood cleanups, and do-it-yourself tenement and brownstone renovations. New Yorkers were dealing with the city's plight in myriad ways. Barlow's article served as a clarion call for action, and the public response was immediate, with donations and offers of volunteer time flowing in.[9]

Brooke Astor provided a grant for the first stage of a master plan to restore the park, mostly focused on architectural features such as Belvedere Castle and the Dairy. Iphigene Sulzberger funded a program to hire kids for summer jobs to help clean up the park. Barlow was hired to run the volunteer program, called the Central Park Task Force. Mayor Koch appointed Gordon Davis the new parks commissioner. Davis had served in different governmental capacities since the administration of John Lindsay, and he immediately turned his attention to Central Park as well.

The Central Park Conservancy emerged, as Gordon Davis explained, through a process on which Joan's input was formative. "During my first month at Parks," Davis told me in an interview at his law office in Midtown Manhattan, "Richard Gilder and George Soros came to introduce themselves and to tell me about the Central Park Community Fund they established to raise private money for Central Park."[10] The park touched twelve different districts, and each had its own park foreman. "The park needs one person in charge of it all, they suggested," Davis recalled. "But I was just on the job. I thanked them but did not focus on it." Then reality seeped in. "I could have spent my entire life focused on Central Park," Davis noted. "Everything was a disaster and there was no money anywhere."

Over several months, Davis got to know "the guardian angels of the park," the people interested in helping financially and who were involved with the four different organizations that had formed to support the effort. Assorted donations were coming in for specific projects, but Davis wanted one person in charge. He and Joan were friends from civil rights activities, and so he called her—"summoned me," as Joan recalled it—to discuss the creation of a new position in the Parks Department: a Central Park administrator. He asked for and received $35,000 from the Fund to hire Barlow to fill that position. But that was not when Joan's help was most critical, Davis said, because others were also donating to the larger effort.

Davis realized Gilder and Soros had a point and called them back. He understood that the base of funding needed to be expanded to bring in corporate and big donations. The idea of a public-private partnership was born, soon to be called the Central Park Conservancy. But it was complicated. "How to do this without it looking like rich people stealing the park from the public was the challenge," said Davis. He drafted a charter setting out rules and authority for the new group, and asked for feedback from Joan. "She asked to come see me and brought her lawyer, William Josephson," Davis recalled, making it clear that this meeting became a seminal moment. "Their message was that, as drafted, this was indeed a kind of abrupt and unreasonable power grab from the city, too much of a reach. So I kept revising the drafted rules and principles. Joan became the test on how to make it acceptable. She kept pushing back. 'Too complicated,' she said. Finally, I said, 'No piece of paper.' This would simply be a new organization to help raise private money for the park, with no clarion declaration of principles that might be misinterpreted." William Beinecke became chair, Davis explained, and went to Mayor Koch and asked only for a promise that the city would not reduce its normal funding for Central Park, which it did anyway as private money came in. "That was a very important moment, and eventually, as things evolved," Davis added pointedly, "the conservancy *earned* a lease with the city. If we had started out with an agreement about powers, it never would have worked."

With Barlow as its first director, the conservancy turned into a widely celebrated success, gained worldwide attention, and helped other cities focus attention on their parks. Early Fund support went, as well, to the Prospect Park Alliance, the Riverside Park Fund, and the City Parks Foundation, which partners with the city to support under-resourced parks in all five boroughs. The public-private partnership concept was still new, and the Central Park Conservancy became the model going forward.

For the conservancy, as for many Fund-supported efforts, it was not the monetary contribution that had its biggest impact. Some projects have marked the beginning of something that grew to national proportions. Some were meant to give credibility to new efforts so other funders would step in. And some offered lessons for top-down policy planners who had ignored—and still do—what is clear to nonexperts: that small interventions add up to big change.

## SMALL PROJECT, BIG LESSON

Many of those big-impact, small-scale investments by the Fund remain, for the most part, unknown. There is no better example of how some of the smallest, most seemingly insignificant grants can bring the biggest results than a $1,500 Fund grant to the Beachside Bungalow Preservation Association, an obscure organization of a handful of local residents in Far Rockaway. In 1992, the group asked for and received a grant to plant thirty trees as well as beach grass, beach plums, bayberry bushes, and other salt-tolerant shrubs behind a small section of beach at

The preservation effort around the 1920s Rockaway bungalows and their beachfront is a great example of the kind of small project with big lessons that the J.M. Kaplan Fund often supported.
CREDIT: HISTORIC DISTRICTS COUNCIL

Far Rockaway, the farthest oceanfront section of Queens.[11] The association had been organized in 1984 to advocate for protection of a small number of surviving 1920s bungalows. This was clearly still a low point for the neighborhood, even though the larger city was on the upswing. The closing of the Long Island Rail Road Rockaway Beach line in the 1950s and widespread demolition during the heyday of Moses's urban-renewal efforts meant there were less than one hundred remaining unheated bungalows out of more than one thousand that had been there. Crime and decay surrounded the enclave. Tony Wood remembered vividly his first site visit. "I took the A train. Halfway there I took off my jacket and tie. When I got off the train in the Rockaways, I took off my watch and rings. As I walked through the neighborhood, there was a trash can on fire and abandoned storefronts with garbage in front, and then I got to Richard George's block, a historic oasis of the cutest bungalows you ever saw—just steps away from an incredible beach. Today, it is no longer an oasis in the urban desert." Considerable new development surrounds the area.

Built in 1921 with uniform facades, compact interiors, generous porches, and exposed rafters, these modest homes had remained affordable to city dwellers. But the oceanfront was precarious, so the association sought plantings that would protect the homes from the encroaching ocean. And protect them they did. In 2012, when Hurricane Sandy devastated the city, particularly along Lower Manhattan and its oceanfront shoreline, this little enclave—with its Fund-supported full-grown trees, beach grass, and double dunes—was spared. A wave broke through one small spot at the end of the storm, bringing one foot of water, reported Richard George, who has spearheaded the neighborhood effort for years. Neighboring communities to both the east and west were flooded with fifteen feet of water, he added, to emphasize how successfully protective the modest plantings had been. In 2009, the HBO series *Boardwalk Empire* filmed the bungalows for its opening shots, and Martin Scorsese donated $10,000.

In the wake of Sandy, no official or professional organization studied the big implications of this modest effort. The dune area was part of Mayor Bloomberg's "Sandy success stories" and an article appeared in *Orion Magazine*, "The City and the Sea." There were bus trips to see the aftermath of Sandy along the Rockaway Peninsula—with a specific stop at the dunes for a walking tour—for students and professors from Harvard, NYU, Columbia, University of Massachusetts, and the Dutch consulate, spearheaded by Walter Meyer, an urban designer based in Brooklyn. At least academics thought this success was worthy of study, but no one from any branch of government joined them.

It gets worse. All that greenery, those twenty-year-old trees, those double dunes, were all destroyed by a thoughtless, out-of-control construction contractor and governmental agencies focused on separate jobs. They could have worked around the existing greenery, but they destroyed it instead. First came the important Army Corps of Engineers dredging project in 2015, meant to move sand from the water to build up the sand on the ocean side of the boardwalk. But, in doing so, the corps bulldozed and removed the established dunes, along with the black pine trees, bayberry bushes, and beach grass planted by Richard George's Beachside Bungalow Preservation Association in 1996 with help from the Parks Department.[12]

Then came the demolition of the old boardwalk in 2016 to make way for a new one. The construction company, Skanska, cut all the black pine trees, bayberry bushes, and *Rosa rugosa* plantings on the north side of the boardwalk, originally planted with help from the J.M. Kaplan Fund and a New York State tree-planting grant. George is now tirelessly pushing every agency involved to repair the damage, although twenty years of growth is hard to bring back quickly. Promises have come from different agencies to replant everything. Only time will tell if any of the agencies live up to their vow to restore the citizens' great work.

George is a classic example of what I call a "citizen planner." With no prior experience, activists like him are forced to learn the system, the laws, the necessary connections, and more. They are committed and determined and know the locality—its condition, character, and needs—better than any professional, but are often ignored or disrespected because they don't have the system-required credential.[13] Tony Wood likened them to the "jailhouse activist lawyer." "Just as inmates in jail often become self-taught legal experts to advance their own case," he noted, "time and again neighborhood activists become self-taught preservation/zoning/environmental legal experts. You can see how these types appealed to the Fund's instincts."

One project above all speaks volumes about the organic rebirth of the city, particularly in the South Bronx. Nineteen seventy-seven was the year of the Yankee game during which radio announcer Howard Cosell spotted a building on fire in the distance and announced to the audience, "The Bronx is burning." Many buildings in the neighborhood were set on fire by arsonists hired by landlords cashing in on insurance policies, or even by tenants for various reasons. Almost everyone had given up hope. The South Bronx had never recovered from the destructive impact of the construction, under Robert Moses, of the Cross Bronx Expressway, which tore through so many stable, integrated, middle-class neighborhoods that the negative impact spread near and far.[14]

Few people anywhere thought recovery was possible. But there were die-hard locals determined to make renewal happen.[15]

Among them was a coalition of citizens seeking to clean up a stretch of the Bronx River that had become a dumping ground for all manner of garbage. The Fund gave the first grant to a small number of believers who were determined to clean up the river, one segment at a time. The Bronx River Restoration Project, a Fund grantee, cleaned the shoreline of debris and overgrowth to create mini parks, pathways, and community gardens, while holding festivals to bring residents to discover the river. The river runs about twenty-four miles, from upper Westchester County to the East River and, like most of the borough in 1977, seemed hopeless. The effort's multiple groups and individuals evolved into the Bronx River Alliance under the strong leadership of Linda Cox. With multiyear Fund support and the support of many others, the alliance has created twenty-three miles of greenway and acres of new and restored parks.

## BEYOND THE CITY

Over the years, the Fund has maintained an ongoing commitment to nature in different guises. It was an early interest of J.M.'s. His attachment to the green countryside emerged first in his days in Cuban sugar fields and then through his deep involvement in the farms and orchards of New York State. Protecting land was an early commitment in the 1950s, and the Fund bought land upstate, especially in the watershed area (see Chapter 7), which protects the city's drinking source.

The Fund's interest in land issues went in several geographical directions beyond the city. There were grants to the Institute for Architecture and Urban Studies to study and prepare a plan for saving Long Island farming as an economic contributor to New York State. The Nature Conservancy received money to acquire the Double Dunes property in East Hampton to prevent private development. J.M. and the family had second homes in East Hampton, where he protected other land from future development.[16] The Group for America's South Fork received money to help protect farms and wetlands in Water Mill. This was all in the 1970s, when the issues of land, wetlands, and shore protection were just heating up.

For a number of years in the 1970s, Joan served on the board of the Nature Conservancy. She was a great supporter of its celebrated director, Pat Noonan. "I admired the ingenious ways he developed to acquire and conserve land," Joan recalled, "and I learned about land trusts from him. We have been a big supporter of land trusts, sometimes buying of easements on farm land to assure the future of farms."[17] The Fund created the New York State Land Trust Alliance, an early statewide effort that proliferated around the country.

A J.M. Kaplan Fund feasibility study grant made possible the opening of a Montessori school in the restored and reclaimed 1905 Crandall barn, a long-vacant former carriage house with a locally produced terra-cotta tile roof.
CREDIT: CAROL A. PRIGMORE

The biggest Fund program outside of the city to preserve both rural land and small communities, called Rural New York, came after J.M.'s death. The program was established by Joan, with Tony Wood, to honor J.M.'s commitment to issues upstate and preserving land, and because the Fund had been in large part financed by the sale of Welch's to upstate grape farmers. "When we started it," Joan said, "I thought it should be named in honor of my father, because his grape industry grew out of the rural country of western New York. So we say Rural New York is recognition of how much he got from the state and how important the state was to him, especially having grown up in the slums of Lowell, Massachusetts. That went on for quite a while and helped inform my thinking when I established Furthermore, a subsidiary of the J.M. Kaplan Fund, in 1995 with an interest in regional publishing." Rural New York simply extended statewide many of the same interests that the Fund had advanced in the city: preservation, land-use planning, open space, and environmental activism on a local scale.

The Rural New York program reflects another trademark of the Fund, a talent to "get into the weeds," as Tony Wood said. This means getting down to the ultimate micro level in a way most foundations try to avoid. To figure out what the program should look like, Wood traveled around the state checking out the local needs that, if met, could have great impacts and scouting for potential grant applicants.

Joan had "fallen in love with the state" when she traveled around it as chairman of the New York State Council on the Arts under Governor Hugh Carey in the mid-1970s. "I was a city girl," she recalled with a laugh. "What did I know about the vast Empire State?" The afterglow of those travels was clearly the inspiration for the Rural New York program. Her guidance was key, but it was now time for Wood to fall in love with upstate as well—and fall in love he did. He wrote detailed trip reports about where he went, who he talked to, and where the Fund could help. In his first report in July 1990, he started in Westport, New York, and opened with: "I had forgotten that heaven was only four and a half hours from New York and located along the shore of Lake Champlain."

His mood stayed lifted from there. Wood went to hamlets and villages in the Adirondacks. He saw how rural cultural grants could be potentially synonymous with economic development grants. He observed the successful combination of affordable housing and senior housing with the preservation of empty historical structures like former hotels or schools. He found that libraries, often in historic buildings, were the anchors of many small communities, doubling effectively as community centers. He discovered how important Fort Ticonderoga was in a region where closed paper mills had undermined the local economy, and he was surprised so little attention had been paid to the Great Camps of the Adirondacks, those luxurious vacation homes built for the rich during the Gilded Age. Constructed of local stone, logs, and shingled roofs and furnished with handmade stick furniture, these assemblages of structures are a uniquely American architectural form, but had never been surveyed. He found towns without zoning facing new development pressures, others fighting badly conceived state transportation road projects that would surely undermine, if not destroy, the local economic, social, and cultural life.

Everywhere, once-significant but now derelict buildings were important to local history, culture, and residents. And there were "the rolling hills and the working landscapes" that were "picture perfect," but where land-trust issues, watershed problems, and wildlife sanctuaries dominated local concerns. Eaton, Moriah, Wadhams, Keeseville—an endless number of places that most downstaters had never heard of, let alone visited. This was 1990, long before the organic farm, farmers' markets, and locally sourced restaurant trends took hold. There was plenty of work to be done, and Joan wanted Wood to figure out how best for the Fund to get involved.

"Everywhere, we went to people we trusted who knew what we were interested in and would help find places and people for us," Wood recalled. Again, it was small grants to be invested in local people or organizations with a good idea and the capacity to pull it off. Yet, the program presented a new challenge for the New York City–based Fund: how to bring all these hyper-local, small-sized grants, all so geographically dispersed, to the Fund's board of trustees, all of whom had a lot of other proposals to digest. There were too many, and the issues involved were too specific and nuanced to cogently present to the board without taking endless hours.

So at Wood's suggestion, with Joan's enthusiastic encouragement, the program was turned into a regrant program, with $100,000 going to each of four statewide groups: the Preservation League of New York State, the Planning Federation, the Open Space Institute, and the Land Trust Alliance.[18] The Fund shaped the program and wrote the ground rules for its operation. Wood oversaw the four groups' management of the process but did not get into the grant evaluation and selection. Projects varied from funding a certified laboratory to monitor water quality to local efforts to challenge the state's decision to locate an incinerator too close to a village. Farmland was saved in perpetuity. Restoration efforts helped local landmark buildings, from Grange halls to historic schools, convert to new uses. Main Streets threatened by new suburban malls were assisted in their revitalization efforts. Studies by conservation groups to demonstrate economic value of natural resources were supported. Dozens of publications, informational videos, maps, exhibits, and brochures were created to promote these diverse local efforts. It is not possible to measure the full effect of this geographically and thematically broad program, but clearly the 598 grants issued from 1993 to 1998, totaling $1.86 million, had an impact larger than their individual parts.

Beyond the planned upstate ventures, Joan was quick to respond in 1989 to an emergency call from Peter Brink, then the new vice president for programs at the National Trust for Historic Preservation. Brink had been alerted by Henry McCartney, executive director of the fledgling Preservation Buffalo Niagara, that the 1895 Roycroft Inn and its campus in East Aurora were in danger of destruction. The inn is where Elbert Hubbard founded the Roycroft artisan community, known for its arts and crafts furniture, light fixtures, pottery, fabrics, books, and more. Empty, in disrepair, and with no prospects for new ownership, the inn and its campus of buildings and workshops—all so important in the history of the arts and crafts movement—was on the brink of falling beyond repair. A $50,000 Fund challenge grant enabled McCartney to reach out to the Wendt Foundation of Buffalo, which donated several million dollars over five years to fully restore the inn and put it back into operation. This success also strengthened McCartney's effort to build Preservation Buffalo Niagara into a significant regional nonprofit.

## RICHARD KAPLAN INITIATED
## ADDITIONAL PROJECTS

From a Harlem vest-pocket park to a historic upstate inn, if the proposal resonated and the people behind it were enthusiastic, energetic, and determined, the J.M. Kaplan Fund could usually be counted on to come through. This was true as well for a favorite program initiated and led by the late Richard Kaplan, Joan's brother.[19] Richard had the same warm smile and the same attraction to the new, the innovative, and, occasionally, the controversial, that Joan has. In the late 1980s and early '90s, Lower Manhattan was suffering from the effects of the 1987 stock market crash, the savings-and-loan crisis, and a recession in real estate markets that produced, in 1994, a vacancy rate above 30 percent. The iconic economic heart of the city and country was not yet witnessing any of the slow, organic rebirth unfolding in other parts of the city.

Richard first wanted to focus on zoning and tax policy that could stimulate renewed interest in downtown. He commissioned a 3D computer model of Lower Manhattan by architect and planner Michael Kwartler, director of the Kaplan-funded Environmental Simulation Lab at the New School, which was to be used in part to study how these kinds of policy changes could be used to revitalize a neighborhood. The Environmental Simulation Lab was an early version of what today is more easily done on computers. It required building a scale model of a place, pasted with actual photos of the buildings. Then a tiny camera floated down the street, creating very real-looking versions of what a street would look like if various city policies were put in place. This technique originated with a lab in Berkeley, California, and the Fund at Richard's behest helped bring it to NYC. It was first used by the Municipal Art Society in the battle over new high-rises proposed for Times Square and again later in the battle over Donald Trump's proposed Upper West Side Television City (Chapter 5).

But what gained more attention was Richard's revival and expansion in 2001 of a bicentennial heritage trail project that had been originally formulated in 1976 but never brought to fruition. Lower Manhattan below Canal Street was already a fully functioning section of the city when, in 1810, the grid was laid out to the north, with a clear crisscrossing of numbered streets and avenues. Thus, historic Lower Manhattan retained its haphazard grid with angled streets—some short, some long—that made finding one's way difficult. There is no clear east-west corridor, so getting from one destination to another was a challenge. Directional signage was nonexistent and, for tourists, finding a destination was impossible. Heritage Trails was meant to help all kinds of pedestrians, local and foreign.

In the late 1990s, this historic area was still suffering from a long decline. Historic walking tours and self-guided trails could be a draw for visitors, especially to an area not experiencing robust activity. The planned trail, with markers in front

Map of Heritage Trails New York, a system of wayfinding in Lower Manhattan that was started and championed by Richard Kaplan
Credit: Courtesy of the Skyscraper Museum

of historic sites and buildings, included themes ranging from archeology to architecture, from Indian walking paths to African burial grounds, from government patrimony to individualist entrepreneurship and international trade. "The concept was, perhaps, overly ambitious, since installing anything on city streets requires a many-step, cumbersome process involving several city agencies from whom approval is required," said Alexia Lalli, the executive director of the project. Over time, about forty markers, including maps and thumbnail histories, were installed, essentially completing the project, and it was turned over to the Downtown Alliance.

Some of the markers were updated, modestly maintained, and lasted for years. The original World Trade Center sign survives as the entry exhibit of the National September 11 Memorial and Museum. "Remember," added Lalli, "this was before everyone had apps on their phone, and Lower Manhattan was not a thriving destination for many tourists or business people." By 2000 the program shut down. But the history of the project—with some very appealing additional material, including sidewalk maps—has been reconstructed by Carol Willis and the Skyscraper Museum.[20] In the end, as the project unfolded, so did the rebirth of Lower Manhattan, which has been transformed from a strictly business district to a twenty-four-hour community of businesses, residents, and cultural attractions.

Richard's most active involvement was with the Regional Plan Association (RPA), where he served on the executive committee for many years. Former president Robert Yaro told me that "Richard showed a remarkable zest and enthusiasm, especially in the early stages of a new idea." Yaro added with a laugh, "The crazier the idea the better." Just like Joan, Richard was receptive to new, untried, and even long-shot ideas that few funders found easy to support. He directed his energy mostly to urban design and transportation challenges.

When Yaro wanted to bring the new chairman of the City Planning Commission, Amanda Burden, and the new transportation commissioner, Janette Sadik-Khan, with him to Copenhagen to visit world-renowned Danish architect Jan Gehl and see how he had transformed that city with decreased parking, increased biking, and inviting public spaces, Richard didn't hesitate to agree to fund the trip. "All he asked was, 'What do you need?'" Yaro said. When RPA was resisting Mayor Bloomberg's call to build a Jets football stadium on the West Side, "Richard stood firm in opposition. It was a contentious issue and a number of board members and contributors ran for cover in the face of phone calls from the mayor's office." When the Metropolitan Transportation Authority was ready to turn over property at the West Side rail yards to the Jets, Yaro and RPA staff "insisted on an appraisal of the land" and Richard backed them up. "When Richard gave us seed money for something," Yaro added, "it always helped to get others to come forward as well."

Richard was also an early supporter of the Civic Alliance to Rebuild Downtown New York, the broad coalition of civic, community, and business groups that RPA convened to advance rebuilding plans for the World Trade Center following the 9/11 terrorist attacks. This led to other major foundations supporting the alliance's work and its "Listening to the City" forums, which brought thousands of New Yorkers into the planning process. The result was an improved rebuilding plan for the World Trade Center site and for the rest of Lower Manhattan—a place that Richard loved.

Parks, public spaces, urban design, and transit were all familiar themes for the Fund, and Richard was as interested and enthusiastic as he could be. The organization's green thumb started with J.M., but it expanded over the years in many different directions as it inevitably should when one's interest is in the whole health of the city.

# 7

## STORM KING, THE RIVER, AND THE HUDSON VALLEY

### *The Environmental Movement Takes Hold*

> Who looks upon a river in a meditative hour, and is
> not reminded of the flux of all things?
> —Ralph Waldo Emerson, *Nature*

B ig change usually begins when citizens come together to
resist a harmful plan. That is exactly how the fight started
in 1963 against a Con Ed plan that would have ripped away
a portion of Storm King Mountain, one of the most dramatic
sites on the Hudson River. The plan would have endangered
the Black Rock Forest on top of the mountain and dramatically undermined the spawning ground for the recreationally
and commercially important striped bass, not to mention the
frightening prospect that it could have turned the Hudson
into an industrialized and damaged waterway that would be
hard to turn around.[1] By the time the fight was over seventeen
years later, a precedent had been established that individuals
could sue on behalf of the public interest in the preservation
and beautification of the natural environment (a transformative

moment in the development of environmental law); Scenic Hudson and the Natural Resources Defense Council had been established; and an awakened public interest in protecting the river's natural and built environment had helped assure that future government policies would reflect the public's attitude.[2]

The first civic initiators of this long, uphill fight—which included many adverse court and governmental decisions—were Steve Duggan and Beatrice Abbott Duggan. The Duggans owned a home in Cornwall, a town on the west bank of the river not far from the site. They had donated a nearby lake for a water-supply reservoir that would have been needed by the power plant. Beatrice, known as Smokey, wrote a letter in March 1964 to the *New York Times*: "If Consolidated Edison is not immediately halted, irrevocable damage will be done to one of the outstanding landmarks of the East on the glorious Hudson River."[3]

"In the beginning, she was a lone voice crying in the wilderness, even signing her maiden name to the letter to protect the reputation of her husband, Stephen Duggan, a partner at the white-shoe Wall Street law firm Simpson, Thacher, and Bartlett," writes John Adams, the first executive director of NRDC.[4] But neighbors soon joined in to organize the 1963 Scenic Hudson Preservation Conference that would put the spotlight on the problem and to launch a lawsuit to protect Storm King. This was an unprecedented citizen undertaking.[5] It was also the launch of Scenic Hudson, an organization that would gain formidable influence in the Hudson Valley.

Franny Reese was another New York City resident with a weekend home near the proposed power plant, although she

CON EDISON'S PROPOSED HYDROELECTRIC PROJECT, CORNWALL, NEW YORK

The pristine Storm King Mountain on the Hudson River and the hydro-power station that Con Ed wanted to insert into the mountain in 1963. The proposal was successfully defeated by a consortium headed by the young NRDC, of which the J.M. Kaplan Fund was a major funder.

CREDIT: SCENIC HUDSON COLLECTION, ARCHIVES & SPECIAL COLLECTIONS, MARIST COLLEGE, USA

was in a community on the east side of the Hudson. Growing up, Franny and her family spent a lot of time camping deep in the wilderness, giving her a strong appreciation for nature. She also learned that when you leave the woods, you should never leave anything behind and always treat nature with respect. So in 1964, she was horrified when she went to a public hearing about Con Ed's plans. She joined the new Scenic Hudson group immediately. A year later, Reese volunteered at Scenic Hudson and eventually became its principal fundraiser and, as

Al Butzel said, "a good deal more, the workhorse of the organization getting off the ground."

"She became perhaps the main mover," Joan reported and others have confirmed. "She dragged us all in happily," Joan added, noting that she had recently returned from living in Oregon and Alaska for twelve years and that the Fund contributed to Reese's hiring. "Franny was a friend of mine in the city," Joan added, "and it was she who first sounded the alarm and organized the early meetings. Everyone realized how environmentally undesirable this would be and how hideous it was." Ray Rubinow, with J.M. and Joan's agreement, signed the Fund on early to this long, expensive legal fight that became one of the most significant moments in the birth of the environmental movement on the East Coast. The Storm King battle and eventual resolution were, effectively, the beginning of the revitalization of the 315-mile Hudson River, often considered the original gateway to the West, and an important starting point in the evolution of modern environmental law.[6]

Clearly, it had been the Hudson River school of painters and writers of the nineteenth century who had brought the river and its exquisite natural environment to public attention. Before the painters romanticized the landscape, people had turned their back on the river they considered dirty. But once the painters brought it to the public consciousness, the Hudson was considered the Rhine of the New World. "The river that flows two ways," Native Americans called it, because salt water from the ocean's tide flowed up the river for 150 miles to Troy—the water brackish for the first forty miles to the Hudson Highlands from the city—and fresh water from the Adirondacks flowed down, the definition of an estuary. "The Lordly Hudson" is what Washington Irving called it, as he looked toward the Catskill Mountains. How could one not respond to the romantic views of the river, waterfalls, and mountains and, at the same time, share concern about the early industrialization of the river, with its coal-fired cement and brick factories, power stations, and other water-polluting industries?

The artists were all, in fact, reacting against the Europeans who had come before, who had acted as though nature were the enemy, cutting down trees and killing animals with abandon. By the time the nineteenth century dawned, people were repulsed by what they saw happening. The paintings of Thomas Cole, Frederic E. Church, Asher B. Durand, Albert Bierstadt, and a host of others, plus the writing of Washington Irving, James Fenimore Cooper, and William Cullen Bryant, all celebrated the beauty and value of nature in general and the river specifically and inspired the early conservation movement, which predated the environmental movement.

"They saw in nature the essence of the country and God, the spirit of America," observed Kent Barwick. Barwick, an early volunteer at the South Street Seaport, of which Joan was a founding supporter, connected the story of the Seaport to that of the river, with the Seaport being one of the earliest building blocks for the country and the river being its first major transportation route, before trains went through the Mohawk Valley and then across America. The opening of the Erie Canal in 1825 provided a direct route to the Great Lakes. Bricks, bells, stoves, horseshoes, and more were produced along the river and shipped off to America's heartland. "And so the Hudson

River Valley, taken in combination with the Mohawk Valley, made America what it is," Barwick continued. "At first, America was a little tiny thing like Rhode Island, between the mountains and the sea, until they figured out how to get inland. So the point is that it wasn't just that the Hudson was celebrated aesthetically, it was historically the most significant quarter in America. And a lot of our history happened here in the revolution, ideas, cultures, new immigrants, music— everything flowed up and down this river."

Barwick pointed out further that the Hudson and Mohawk Valleys played an important part in World War II. "It's just amazing what was going on," he said. "This is where a lot was built and produced: rifles, tanks, ammunition, the underwear for troops, the socks, the bandages, the lifeboats, everything was produced here. The lowest moment came after the war when factories started to move south."

With all that industrialization came increasing pollution. The river was filled with raw sewage, toxic chemicals, and oil pollution. Fish were disappearing. The Con Ed proposal seemed to be the breaking point. It would have been the largest pump storage hydroelectric project in the world, carved into Storm King Mountain, extending 800 feet along the shore and rising 110 feet above the Hudson, leaving a gash the size of three football fields laid end to end.[7] While there was little precedent for citizen opposition to this kind of massive project, more people started saying not only that enough was enough but that the long-standing industrial trend had to be reversed.

Over the years, an interesting assortment of organizations had emerged to defend the river, with little to show for their efforts. All of them can be found in the yearly lists of grants of the J.M. Kaplan Fund, reflecting the early interest—first of J.M. and then of Ray Rubinow and Joan—in preserving both the natural and built environment. But it wasn't until the collective efforts of these organizations came under the umbrella of the lawsuit that a reversal of the negative trend began and new and potent defenders emerged.

David Sampson, first executive director of the Hudson River Greenway, maintains that "America's environmental movement began in the Hudson River Valley—twice. The artists of the early 1800s initiated the first time by showing Europeans—and Americans—an American landscape of beauty, not the dark forested lands that came with the Puritan vision of America."[8]

An early organization of fishermen, for example, was founded in the 1960s to bring attention to the tiny fish being killed by the water-intake equipment installed at one of Con Ed's existing nuclear plants, at Indian Point in Westchester County. This kicked off the second phase of the environmental movement on the Hudson. Founded in 1966 by Robert H. Boyle, a sportswriter and avid fisherman, the Hudson River Fishermen's Association (which eventually became Riverkeeper) successfully went after polluters of all kinds, including the Penn Central railroad, whose train oil was spewing into the river.[9] Boyle liked to point out that the Hudson was the only estuary on the Atlantic coast of the United States that still retained all its original fish species.[10] He also warned early about polychlorinated biphenyl (PCB) coming into the river from various sources. Boyle, author of the highly acclaimed 1969 *The Hudson River: A Natural and Unnatural History*, became "the

Musician Pete Seeger led the effort to develop the *Clearwater*, a 109-foot replica of the sloops that sailed the Hudson in the eighteenth and nineteenth centuries, as a way to bring awareness to the threats to the river.
CREDIT: ECONOSMITH.COM

unofficial guardian of the Hudson River as a crusading conservationist," Sam Roberts writes in Boyle's *New York Times* obituary on May 22, 2017.

In 1966, legendary musician and activist Pete Seeger announced plans to "build a boat to save the river." The *Clearwater*, for which the J.M. Kaplan Fund was an early funder, was a 109-foot replica of the sloops that sailed the Hudson in the eighteenth and nineteenth centuries. Seeger envisioned it as an educational opportunity to bring people to the river, where they could experience its multifaceted beauty and be moved to work to save it.

All the well-researched and persuasive evidence of damage and all the grassroots opposition were not enough to persuade the Federal Power Commission (FPC) to deny Con Ed the permit to build the power plant in 1965. A lawsuit was the only recourse. Hopeless as it may have seemed, Lloyd K. Garrison, a lawyer who cared deeply about the natural world in general and the Hudson in particular, was persuaded to take the case.[11] His partner, Judge Simon Rifkind, a renowned trial and appellate attorney, was persuaded as well.[12] Garrison assigned the case to Al Butzel, his new young assistant at Paul, Weiss, Rifkind, Wharton & Garrison.

As Butzel, who remained lead litigator of the Storm King case for fifteen years, writes:

There was no such thing as environmentalism at the time, but there was a long history of conservation—a good deal of which emanated from New York and the Hudson River. It is no accident that Theodore Roosevelt was a New Yorker. It is no accident that J.P. Morgan, Colonel Ruppert, the Rockefellers, the Harrimans, the Perkins, and many other wealthy families built their summer homes in the Hudson Highlands. Nor is it serendipity that the Adirondacks were declared "forever wild" at the insistence of New York City families in 1892, or that in 1910, Charles Evans Hughes, then Governor of New York and later Chief Justice of the Supreme Court, signed into law an extension for the Palisades Park to include the Highlands as far north as Newburgh. John Muir may have founded the conservation movement, but it was the wealth of New York City—and the interest of its patricians—that fueled it. It should, then, be no surprise that Lloyd Garrison, great-grandson of the abolitionist William Lloyd Garrison, himself a New Yorker by heritage, cared about the land and believed in conservation. So when he was asked to take an appeal to the Second Circuit, there was no way he was going to say no.[13]

Conservation indeed had a long history before the mid-1960s, having emerged in the late 1800s, driven by such wilderness lovers as Ralph Waldo Emerson, Henry David Thoreau, and the Hudson Valley's own John Burroughs. John Muir founded the Sierra Club in San Francisco in 1892. Then came Theodore Roosevelt, Gifford Pinchot, the establishment of the US Forest Service, and the founding of the National Audubon Society. The National Park Service was created in 1916, the Wilderness Society in 1935, and the National Wildlife Federation in 1936—all mostly concerned with saving natural places and wild animals.

But the 1960s saw devastating oil spills like that off the coast of Santa Barbara, air pollution alerts, the Cuyahoga River on fire, and raw sewage despoiling pristine waters. In 1962, Rachel Carson's *Silent Spring* was published and a national environmental consciousness came into being. The first version of the Clean Air Act was passed in 1963.[14] Plans to dam the Glen Canyon, upstream from the Grand Canyon, and David Brower and the Sierra Club's vigorous fight against the damming, were generating a lot of new interest. The National Environmental Policy Act was passed in 1969, requiring environmental assessments and impact statements for all projects involving federal actions, funding, or permits. Resistance was growing to the new interstate highways that were slashing through both much-loved nature and urban neighborhoods. Even President Lyndon B. Johnson spoke of the natural landscape as a "quality of life" issue in his 1965 State of the Union address, saying:

> For over three centuries, the beauty of America has sustained our spirit and enlarged our vision. We must act now to protect this heritage. In a fruitful new partnership with the States and the cities the next decade should be a conservation milestone. We must make a massive effort to save the countryside and establish—as a green legacy for tomorrow—more large and small parks, more seashores and open spaces than have been created during any other period in our national history.[15]

The National Historic Preservation Act was passed by Congress in 1966, seeking protection for the built heritage that was falling under the wrecking ball of urban renewal and highway building. Also that year, Olana, the 1870 Victorian home of Frederic E. Church near the city of Hudson, was acquired by New York State and in 1967 designated a national historic site after a long rescue effort.[16] "So all those things were happening," NRDC lawyer Eric Goldstein said, "and then it exploded with Earth Day, the first Earth Day, where tens of millions turned out on April 22, 1970." A new national awareness about all aspects of the environment was growing. It was not as if nature organizations were not around until then, Goldstein was quick to point out. "Some would do occasional lobbying, but most didn't have an ongoing congressional presence," he added. "For example, the Sierra Club had been around for years but it was only in the '60s that it opened an office in Washington, DC. Environmental Defense Fund was formed in 1967 by scientists out on Long Island who were concerned about the toxic pesticide DDT. So a lot was developing in the '60s and it exploded in the '70s."

It may be that the fight for Storm King Mountain came at the right time. Scenic Hudson's already expensive lawsuit was stalling the project, although the FPC showed no sympathy for the opposition.[17] "There was not a huge constituency, but there was a lot of press and Ray Rubinow of the Kaplan Fund was running around the country raising money for the lawsuit and organizing a national fundraising campaign," Butzel told me in an interview in his Manhattan office. It was clearly going to be a long haul. "Between Ray and Franny," Butzel noted, "Storm King became a national cause célèbre." Before that, he said, "interest was waning, so Joan and the Fund came in at a crucial point."

It took seventeen years to resolve the issue. After the Federal Power Commission upheld the granting of the license to construct the Storm King plant, the environmental groups appealed and the US Court of Appeals for the Second Circuit in 1965 issued a landmark ruling. It reversed the FPC action and sent the case back to the commission for further proceedings. In terms of legal principles, the case was historic. For the first time, a federal appeals court had ruled that the plaintiff's "standing" to file a case need not be based solely on personal economic injury, but that the environmental group's interest in "aesthetic, conservational and recreational aspects of power development" was sufficient to allow their case to proceed in court. After years of additional hearings and court rulings, the FPC again upheld the issuance of the license to construct the power plant. But continuing public objections, hearings before other agencies, financial problems at Con Ed, fisheries studies, the possibility of a gas turbine alternative, and further appeals to the FPC had delayed construction. Ultimately, "the Department of the Interior and the Federal Power Commission's own staff came to the conclusion that the plant should not be built," writes Butzel. "The handwriting was on the wall."[18]

But wheels of government move slowly even when stopping something. Five years later, Con Ed surrendered its license, gave the property to the Palisades Interstate Park Commission, and was part of a final settlement that provided for seven other Hudson power plants to install elaborate fish protection. In all, twelve parties were at the negotiating table, and the settlement included $12 million from Con Ed and other utilities to establish a Hudson River Foundation.[19] In 1980, fifteen years after the lawsuit began, the battle was over. However, of great value and significance was the precedent, set by the suit, that a person or group did not have to suffer economic damage to be able to sue, and that just an interest in the environment was enough to provide standing. This, as noted, was the landmark beginning of modern environmental law and activism many commentators have acknowledged.

Early on in the lawsuit, however, Steve Duggan saw the Storm King case as a potential launching pad for a nonprofit environmental law firm. Duggan and lawyers Whitney North

Seymour Jr. and David Sive understood that a singular lawsuit would undoubtedly take years and be unsustainable financially. A new direction was needed, they agreed, one based on what was becoming known as public interest law, which was already emerging to fight for civil rights and the rights of women, children, and the poor.[20] Thus was born the Natural Resources Defense Council, which would focus entirely on litigation on behalf of a broad definition of the environment.[21] Seymour, who went on to be the US attorney for the Southern District of New York, had a young lawyer working for him, John Adams, who was suggested as NRDC's first executive director. It was under Adams's thirty years of leadership that the NRDC became what many consider to be the leading environmental advocacy organization and the formidable global force it is today.

"There was nothing else like it," recalled Joan, who responded to NRDC's founding early. "The Nature Conservancy was a big deal of course, and there were parks groups and Bob Boyle, who was still somewhat unheralded then. The Sierra Club was perceived as a California thing.[22] I was on the board of the Nature Conservancy, and there were some mutterings that they weren't as feisty as needed. And who couldn't love those dashing, energetic young guys who had come together to form NRDC?"

John Adams reached out to Joan early, "when starting an organization to hold polluters accountable in court still seemed like a bizarre idea to many," Adams said. "While we were trying to set up offices, test the idea of citizen lawsuits, and hire staff to help enforce the Clean Air Act and Clean Water Act and other new environmental laws that had just been put on the books, Joan arrived and helped our organization grow and mature. She wasn't one of the original trustees, but she was one of the early ones who really shaped what we were to become."

Joan remembered with pride that, after NRDC was launched with a Ford Foundation grant, the J.M. Kaplan Fund came in with the second grant and she joined the board. Sitting in his kitchen at his Beaverkill Valley farmhouse in the Catskills, John Adams could not say enough good things about Joan—both her financial support and her active involvement in NRDC. "Everything we needed in those early years, Joan delivered," he said. "She was the first big supporter of NRDC's work to protect the Catskill watershed and reservoirs that supply drinking water to half the population of New York State. She understood the importance of preventing pollution and safeguarding the Catskills landscape as a cost-effective watershed-protection strategy, long before many people did, and she enabled NRDC to play a leading role on the issue for decades."

Adams also emphasized Joan's role in pulling NRDC into urban issues through the battle over preserving the Broadway theaters (Chapter 5). "When people talked about protecting the environment in the 1970s, they tended to mean preserving dense forests, rushing rivers, and wild places. But Joan helped us see that cities could be green—that by making cities better, more sustainable places to live, we could help protect the natural systems we all depend on. She came to this understanding through her deep commitment to historic preservation and started NRDC talking about the threat of overdevelopment and destruction of New York City's historical landmarks years before these issues became front-page news. She courageously funded NRDC to hire a team of lawyers led by Mitch Bernard to litigate to protect some of New York's architectural treasures at a time when some people thought NRDC should not get so engaged in city matters."

The watershed issue that Adams referred to was brought to the public's attention in large measure because of a conference pulled together and supported by the Fund. "We gathered all the relevant agencies of the city—water, transportation, planning—and a lot of nonprofits, and Eric Goldstein from NRDC," Joan recalled, remembering the first coming together around the watershed. "I think Eric got rather inspired by the whole meeting and brought it back to NRDC and they then proceeded to wage a long, courageous, and effective campaign."

The Catskill watershed became a huge controversy for years. It supplies about 90 percent of New York City's water, but when the state proposed that the city filter its water in 1990, not many people understood what a singular challenge this would be. The 1986 federal Safe Drinking Water Act required that all surface drinking-water supplies in the country, like lakes and reservoirs, be filtered. By 1990, most public water systems in the country were filtered. The exceptions were localities with a very high-quality water system and a comprehensive watershed-protection program to insure its continued quality. NRDC believed that the "six giant reservoirs west of the Hudson River called the Catskill and Delaware systems did not need to be filtered because the area was still relatively rural," explained Goldstein, who handled this complex issue, in an interview in his NRDC Manhattan office. "We thought, it's better to protect those waters by preserving the watershed land surrounding the reservoirs rather than building what even then would have been a multibillion-dollar filtration plant, which we felt would have removed the incentive and the government focus on preventing pollution in the first place." The city owned very little of the targeted land at that point. In addition to NRDC, the city's Department of Environmental Protection commissioner under Mayor Dinkins, Al Appleton, and Riverkeeper leader Robert F. Kennedy were focused on this issue.

"So we [Adams, Goldstein, Appleton, and Kennedy] met with Joan and Tony [Wood], and they immediately saw the beauty and multiple benefits," Goldstein recalled. "You'd be protecting water quality at its source and preserving forest lands and agriculture—because the key strategy in pollution prevention was land acquisition. And you would be saving New York City ratepayers' funds because this strategy would be less expensive than building a massive filtration plant, which would have been the largest in the nation, if not the world, to treat well over a billion gallons a day of water."

Joan became the main funder of this complicated effort, first to get the state to reverse the filtration order and then to launch a comprehensive watershed-protection program at considerably less cost. In 1992, the Fund treated this as the emergency campaign that the experts said it was and distributed a $560,000 grant among what the annual report calls "seven of New York State's strongest environmental organizations" to help them join forces and save New York's water supply.

This was an extraordinary effort, and it is not clear whether the public, at the time, understood the gravity of the situation. The city's water system had nineteen reservoirs in the Catskill

Mountains and Westchester County, delivering daily over 1.2 billion gallons of drinking water. The water was considered the finest in the nation, but it was under imminent threat from pollution. NRDC and Riverkeeper were in the lead, but all aspects of this complex issue were covered. The Regional Plan Association helped towns, hamlets, and villages initiate plans and institute land-use regulations to address roadway runoff, erosion, and failing sewage and septic systems whose runoff went into streams feeding reservoirs. The Beaverkill Valley Conservancy (an affiliate of the Open Space Institute) and Trust for Public Land bought key parcels of land. Cornell University's New York State Water Resources Institute identified and promoted non-damaging recreation programs in the Catskill State Park. And the Catskill Center for Conservation and Development offered local farmers technical assistance and developed a network of model farm projects to change damaging agricultural practices.

Appleton, representing the city, developed a draft plan with NRDC and Riverkeeper that took nearly a decade to negotiate and finalize with upstate communities in what, as Goldstein described, "was considered a landmark political agreement. Implementation of the ambitious watershed-protection plans continues to this day." Fund support never wavered. As of 2017, Goldstein said, over 140,000 acres of land have been preserved, and sewage plants throughout the watershed have been substantially upgraded, all with city funds. "Total expenses have been less than $2 billion," Goldstein calculated, adding that building a filtration plant would have cost ratepayers $10 billion in capital funds alone.

But that was the Catskill watershed, the larger of the two that serve New York City. As Goldstein explained: "The city's first upstate water source was the Croton system, which went into service in 1842, when the city dammed the Croton River in Westchester County. Unlike the more rural Catskill watershed, the much smaller Croton watershed was increasingly suburbanized post World War II, and water quality in the Croton was threatened. For that reason, the city ended up building a whole other sewage filtration plant [in the Bronx] for the 10 percent of the water east of the Hudson reservoirs. That was originally projected at $750 million and ended up costing over $2.3 billion." Of the million-acre watershed, Goldstein estimated, the state and city combined own nearly 40 percent, a substantial proportion. And while more land could be acquired in the future, this Kaplan-fueled effort increased New York City's watershed landholdings by more than 500 percent.[23]

Goldstein cited this watershed story as a reflection of Joan and the Fund's critical support. He said, "She quickly grasped the boundaries of the battle and understood what the long-term goal was and she supported that with her typical enthusiasm. She would be behind you all the way and with you as a partner on the front lines and ready to take the heat. The heat didn't matter. In fact, I think she enjoyed the heat as well."

The Fund's involvement in watershed-land conservation issues led to strong support for upstate land trusts, whereby property owners can donate the development rights to their open land in exchange for an income-tax deduction. The Trust for Public Land was national, but the Adirondack Land Trust, Open Space Institute, American Farmland Trust, and

Columbia Land Conservancy were focused on saving lands in New York State from unwarranted or damaging development, all supported by the Fund. The interest in land, of course, was something close to the heart of J.M. Kaplan, so it wasn't a stretch for the Fund to find any number of creative ways to preserve open space, whether farmland or watershed property.

One of the NRDC programs of which Joan is also proud is the establishment of the organization's magazine, *Amicus Journal*. She became intimately involved in the founding and long-term support of the publication. "Joan was always ready to take things on," John Adams recalled. "And I mean that's the essence of Joan. And I think she found a like-minded person in me. And she liked what we were doing. Whenever I had an idea, I would talk to her and she would say, yeah I like that, let's do it. That includes starting the magazine."

So by 1979, Joan, Adams, and Pattie Sullivan at NRDC already had a solid history of working together when Adams asked former *Time* magazine journalist Peter Borrelli to suggest what NRDC should do to raise its public profile. "NRDC needed to establish a specific identity," Adams writes in his history of the NRDC. "Being an environmental law firm wasn't enough. We were still small compared to older organizations such as the Sierra Club and the National Audubon Society, and unlike them we didn't have a 'founding father' like John Muir or John James Audubon."[24]

"We had this little dinky newsletter like everyone else," Goldstein explained, "and we said, hey, we want to have a journal of independent thought that puts out creative ideas on the environmental scene and is influential in the halls of Congress."

Borrelli suggested transforming the organization's newsletter into a quarterly journal of thought and opinion. The name, *Amicus Journal*, alluded to the amicus (friend of the court) briefs NRDC filed in various lawsuits. This was 1979, and not many sources of serious environmental journalism were available. "At the Fund, we thought it was a great idea," Joan recalled. "And it wouldn't actually be a mouthpiece for NRDC but would take a broad, critical look at the big environmental issues of the day. And it would be independent, not under NRDC editorial control." In the early years, Joan was involved with every aspect of the magazine. She was on the editorial board, helped set up the rules, and made sure it was independent. "It was a huge success," Adams said. "It put NRDC on the map. We became a voice in our world because of that magazine and we had great writers." In 2002, the magazine name was changed to *onEarth* and went digital only.

## A NEW STATEWIDE INTEREST

By 1978, the Fund had already been supporting a number of upstate issues—primarily environmental ones, like the Storm King fight and aftermath. But there was work to be done upstate in historic preservation that Joan was getting more and more interested in. "We were getting requests for grants that were appealing, and I thought it was time to take a look at what was going on up there in the Hudson River Valley and New York State."

In 1975, at a statewide conference of the Preservation League of New York State at Great Camp Sagamore in the

Adirondacks, Joan had met Wint Aldrich, assistant to the state commissioner of environmental conservation.[25] Winty, as he is known by some, has the rumpled look of a favorite professor, with a warm smile and friendly manner. He is a much-admired fixture in the Hudson Valley and in statewide historic preservation circles, known for his decades of efforts to protect both the natural environment and built heritage. He is a member of the tenth generation of his family to own the sprawling 420-acre Rokeby estate, with its forty-three-room mansion in Barrytown built in 1811 for the Armstrongs, whose daughter married William B. Astor. The blood of almost all the historic Hudson Valley families flows through his veins: Astor, Livingston, Stuyvesant, Fish.

At the conference, Joan sat down next to Aldrich to introduce herself and uttered little hints about seeing Rokeby. They wound up deep in conversation about conservation and preservation, struck up a friendship, and eventually began to focus on the Hudson Valley. Years later, as state parks commissioner, Joan appointed Aldrich to be the agency's first deputy commissioner of historic preservation.

Some of the great landmarks along the Hudson, Aldrich told Joan at dinner, were in trouble or already disappearing. Joan's interest was piqued, and she decided to organize a bus tour from New York City, led by Aldrich, for a mix of people that included J.M. and Alice Kaplan, who were also Fund trustees; people from the press, including me; assorted preservationists; and members of other foundations.[26] Joan was not only interested in how the Fund might get involved in preservation but was also hoping to get others interested as well.

"She was particularly interested in the properties that were at risk," Aldrich recalled in an interview. "That meant we were going to be trudging through some rough ground, so I alerted everyone to be sure to wear sensible shoes." He smiled at the memory of at least one woman showing up in high heels, but "Mr. and Mrs. Kaplan were the only ones who had really listened to me and they came in brand new, red matching sneakers." This was a few years before Joan bought the spectacular Livingston homestead, Midwood, a Victorian vernacular country house on the Hudson near Tivoli, but she was already interested in the valley and wanted her family, friends, and colleagues to be infatuated as well.

This elaborate 1852 Victorian mansion, Wilderstein, was built by Thomas Holy Suckley, one of the Hudson River gentry families.
CREDIT: PHOTOGRAPH BY ROLF MÜLLER

The site on the tour that I remember best was Wilderstein, the seemingly falling-down nineteenth-century Queen Anne pile of turrets, chimneys, and porches overlooking the Hudson in Rhinebeck. At the time, it was still an occupied home. It was built in 1852 by Thomas Holy Suckley, an export trader and real estate magnate related to the Beekmans, Livingstons, and other Hudson River gentry. Still in residence was the last of three generations of Suckleys, Margaret "Daisy" Suckley, a cousin of FDR, whose fancy old clothes still filled the attic.[27] The Fund became an early supporter when Wilderstein was established in 1980 as a historic site after the energetic efforts of Duane Watson.

Not far from Wilderstein, we visited an already long-neglected Wyndcliffe, the 1853 imposing brick castle that had been abandoned decades after the death of its owner, Elizabeth Schermerhorn Jones, a lavish party giver for her high society friends. She is said to be where the expression "keeping up with the Joneses" originated. The house was already crumbling when we visited it and has since collapsed. The tour also stopped at Montgomery Place, the 1805 Federal mansion redesigned and expanded by Alexander Jackson Davis, then owned by John White Delafield and his wife. Kent Barwick recalled house staff "following us around like hawks as if we might steal something." After Delafield's death, the house was owned by a foundation, Historic Hudson Valley, and in 2016 was bought by Bard College, which already had a sprawling riverfront campus adjoining Montgomery Place.

The sites were not all neglected. We also visited Edgewater, the magnificent 1824 home of Richard Jenrette—the

The Rokeby mansion was first built in 1811 in the Federal style, then enlarged in 1858 to include the polygonal tower and mansarded third floor and service wing. In 1894, Stanford White redesigned the interior. CREDIT: HISTORIC AMERICAN BUILDINGS SURVEY (LIBRARY OF CONGRESS)

Wall Street trailblazer and cofounder of Donaldson, Lufkin & Jenrette—who has spent more than forty years buying, restoring, and saving in perpetuity early American great houses. Edgewater—a mélange of classical styles including Doric columns, Roman arched doors, and intricate interior details from various periods—was built by one of the members of the historic Livingston family. The earliest Livingstons arrived from Scotland by way of Holland in the seventeenth century, and over the generations claimed signers of the Declaration of Independence and Constitution, governors, and presidents among their members. Their roots run deep in the Hudson Valley, with thirty or more houses built by and for family members.

The tour was treated, of course, to a visit to Winty Aldrich's beloved Rokeby, which, like historic properties throughout the region, had its financial and preservation challenges. But things here are looking up, Aldrich noted in an interview for this book. "It's just the three of us and the next generation, ten family owners as partners," he said. "But everyone came together and now we have income-producing rental properties." The house and grounds are often the site of nonprofit fundraisers and tours, political rallies, and the like, as well as family reunions and parties for friends. Aldrich said with pride that "it all looks better and is in better physical shape inside and out since we inherited Rokeby fifty years ago."

The June 21, 1978, bus tour turned out to be a kickoff for a new era, when more attention would be paid to the unknown or unrecognized historic sites in the Hudson Valley that now make up a well-visited tourism circuit.[28] "That was my first exposure to the lore and wonders of the Hudson Valley," remembered Margot Wellington, then the executive director of the Municipal Art Society. This was true probably for all of us on the tour. It is difficult to assess what specifically came out of the experience. The tour did get the attention of local river town leaders who, as Aldrich noted, cared little about these historic properties in the late 1970s. A small group of concerned local residents, including Joan's good friend Mike Gladstone, had formed Hudson River Heritage, but they had no ability to do much except care about saving local landmarks. Eventually, a consortium of local governments was formed to help bring these localities together to think about waterfront planning. Of course, the Fund was there to get the process started and nurture it along. "One thing led to another," Aldrich observed, "and now there is great local concern and there has been some super planning and zoning work done."

A few years later, in 1985, Joan bought her own 1887 house, Midwood, on eighty-five acres overlooking the Hudson River. "These grand houses hardly ever came up for sale in those days," Joan said, explaining that, on this rare occasion, she heard about it from friends. "I drove up with a friend on a cold, rainy March day just for a look, never thinking I wanted a country house. As we moseyed down that long romantic driveway, I said, 'Uh-oh.' The house doesn't matter and could be replaced—the setting is all. And then, look! The setting was perfection and the house was too." She bought it and set about imaginatively making this seemingly simple Victorian country house into her new family home. With an amazing ability to throw together rare antiques and tag-sale finds, Joan furnished the house with eclectic aplomb. She expanded the living room, replicating details to make it impossible to know it wasn't original, and had the living room walls hand-painted with decorative elements from ancient Pompei and Boscotrecase. With a special wing added for children's activities, it was a perfect gathering place for her growing family of grandchildren, for whom she provided all the trappings of a summer adventure at "Camp Midwood."

Midwood became a gathering place for many, beyond family ties. A yearly spring shad party—to celebrate the Hudson River fish at the high point of its run—was attended by several hundred of the good people from all of Joan's worlds, upstate and down—a great celebratory occasion and opportunity for networking. This was classic Joan. For her, networking was a high art, whether on the lawn and room-size front porch of Midwood or in the daily comings and goings of Fund activities.

Today, towns along the Hudson are occasionally threatened with the kind of project the Fund would be called on to fight against, like the huge cement plant that a foreign company tried to build on the shore of the city of Hudson. In 2014, the Fund again supported the NRDC's fight against the intrusion of LG's corporate headquarters in the historic Palisades along the Hudson River. This effort, combined with the advocacy of Scenic Hudson and Laurance Rockefeller, successfully reduced the size of the building to the tree line, preserving the historic Hudson River viewshed.

But the towns along the river have evolved into their own mostly successful watchdog, only occasionally turning to the Fund for help. Historic preservation, land conservation, and environmental concerns are front-and-center issues in many communities. All of this is a far cry from the early days, when the Fund, by necessity and instinct, was in the vanguard of the Hudson Valley's protection.

# 8

# TOWARD A
# MORE CIVIL SOCIETY

Running through all the Fund's areas of interest so far has been a subtext of civil rights, civil liberties, and the overall theme of social justice. Are not parks and accessible public spaces about the right of citizens to enjoy free, livable communities? Are not all the citizen-based lawsuits—against destructive highways or excessively high floors, or for saving civically important buildings, preventing destructive, inappropriate development, and saving farmland—about social justice, community rights, and citizen protections? Are not the fights against environmental degradation, highway building, urban destruction, and landmark demolition efforts to make the civic will prevail over the corporate demand? After all, much of the Fund's work has been about quality of life (whether urban or rural), and shouldn't that also be a basic civil right? Even the Supreme Court ruled that cities have the right to regulate on the ground of aesthetics and beauty, as well as public safety.[1]

Civil rights and civil liberties were at the heart of J.M. Kaplan's early interest in the New School. Founded in 1919 by a group of pacifist refugee academics that included Columbia University professors chastised for speaking out against the war, the New School subsequently became a refuge for European intellectuals and academics fleeing fascism and Nazism. With a lot of early support from the Rockefeller Foundation, the New School became known as a "university in exile" as it welcomed scholars and artists fleeing Europe. Its reputation as a "forum for scholars, political activists, and artists to exchange ideas and to react publicly to international events" appealed to J.M.'s political sensibilities, but also to his appreciation for the formal education he never enjoyed.[2] J.M. pursued his own path of education by reading biographies of the likes of Benjamin Franklin, Mark Twain, and Thomas Jefferson, but he also greatly admired the educators drawn to teaching at the New School. Through social contacts, he watched the school's gradual evolution and gave his first grant of $5,000 in 1950 for general support. That quickly accelerated to $10,000 two years later and then $40,000 for general support and help in covering a deficit. From then on, the New School was J.M.'s biggest and longest financial commitment and, as noted earlier, he became chairman of its board. Eventually, he was joined by Albert A. List in spearheading an ambitious building program to accommodate the growing student body.

Starting with support for the mayoral campaign of Fiorello La Guardia, J.M. Kaplan personally contributed to various liberal political candidates, especially the campaign of Adlai Stevenson. Workers' rights and union democracy were another strain of J.M.'s support. With the encouragement of DC lawyer Joseph L. Rauh, whom he greatly admired, J.M. generously supported the Association for Union Democracy, paying for staff lawyers and general support in the fight to overcome corrupt union bosses and provide rank-and-file elections.

J.M.'s commitment to free expression and liberal causes found another outlet in his ambition to start a chain of independent newspapers in small towns across the country, to counter what he saw as the proliferation of conservative, family-owned papers that he felt dominated the political discourse. He went so far as to establish the Community Newspaper Publishers, Inc., but he never got further than starting the *Middletown Daily Record* in Middletown, New York, in 1956. Although it gained a respectable following, it was always in the red, and J.M. sold it to the Gannett chain in 1971.

Starting in the late 1940s, J.M. supported the National Urban League, particularly their voting-registration efforts, and the NAACP Legal Defense and Education Fund, known as the Inc. Fund, which was bringing lawsuits throughout the South to further integration and voter registration. In the 1950s and '60s, the Inc. Fund was at the forefront of lawsuits that moved integration forward in small but groundbreaking steps. Over the years, J.M. particularly supported its projects about prisoners' rights and capital punishment.

Perhaps the Fund's longest commitment to civil rights and civil liberties was J.M. and Joan's interest in the ACLU, starting with J.M.'s first payment of membership dues in 1951. That started a long-lasting commitment, with special grants going to support efforts related to censorship, amnesty, the Freedom of Information Act, reproductive freedom, abortion rights, voting rights, and support for immigration. Much of this support was in the protest years of the 1960s and '70s, when the ACLU was under the acclaimed leadership of Aryeh Neier, the organization's first executive director. Neier, a legendary civil liberties champion, shaped the ACLU into a formidable national force.

Neier has a soft-spoken manner and gentle smile that belie the ferocity of his outsized leadership of the contentious civil liberties and civil rights fields. "Joan was a direct benefactor of mine," he noted in an interview at his Manhattan office at the Open Society Foundations, where he served as director from 1993 to 2012. "She was the first significant funder of Human Rights Watch at $200,000, a year before Ford Foundation came in. She was crucial in launching us." Neier also became the first executive director of Human Rights Watch.

The 1960s and '70s, Neier recalled, were turbulent times for the ACLU, especially with the Vietnam protests. "We represented tens of thousands of demonstrators against the war and draft-card burners, launched new programs dealing with conditions in prisons and a women's rights project." He appointed Ruth Bader Ginsburg the first director of that project. She litigated on behalf of the ACLU until President Jimmy Carter appointed her to the US Court of Appeals in 1980 and then President Bill Clinton appointed her to the US Supreme Court in 1993.

Probably the most contentious issue the ACLU ever faced was its defense of the National Socialist Party of America's right to march in Skokie, Illinois. The neo-Nazis wanted to march in uniforms that would display the swastika. The legal fight led to the US Supreme Court, which upheld a US Court

Joan stood behind the ACLU's First Amendment defense of the National Socialist Party of America's 1977 attempt to march in Skokie, Illinois. The US Supreme Court upheld their right, but the march was moved to Chicago.

of Appeals decision by declining to hear the case. The vote was seven to two. The ACLU lost many supporters over that issue, but "Joan stuck by us, even increasing her donation," Neier said. Most importantly, Neier observed, the Fund's support "was not a huge amount of money but always had a disproportionate positive impact." Speaking of Joan's overall impact on New York City, Neier added: "Joan has a vision of a city that's lively intellectually but preserves attractive features of its past. Unfortunately, her campaigns on behalf of public toilets and for saving the old Scribner's bookstore were a failure, but she was successful with many other things like the Greenmarkets, saving the historic theaters."

Not too many foundations had such a disproportionate impact as the J.M. Kaplan Fund in the 1960s and '70s, Neier said. He cites two others that did: the estate of Marshall Field and the Irene Diamond Fund. The Field Foundation was led by the late Leslie Dunbar, whose focus was civil rights and children. "Field under Dunbar had a great impact on civil rights, racial equality, and voting rights," Neier said. The Field Foundation's financial support was critical for Martin Luther King's Poor People's Campaign and Marian Wright Edelman's fledgling Children's Defense Fund. The Irene Diamond Foundation focused on public health and established the Aaron Diamond AIDS Research Center, which developed the lifesaving antiretroviral therapy that suppresses the HIV virus and halts progression of the disease.

Neier left the ACLU to form Human Rights Watch, and Joan was there from the beginning. A significant book project by the Fund and Human Rights Watch was yet another dramatic example of calling important attention early to a cause: *Forced Out: The Agony of the Refugee in Our Time*, by Carole Kismaric, an innovative editor and book packager, with commentary by William Shawcross, a British journalist and author who later became a member of the UN High Commissioner for Refugees' informal advisory group.[3] The book was published by the Fund, Human Rights Watch, and four major publishers in 1989 to focus on the horrendous refugee crisis of the time.[4] It might just as well have been published today. As Joan said, "We thought it was a horror then that there were

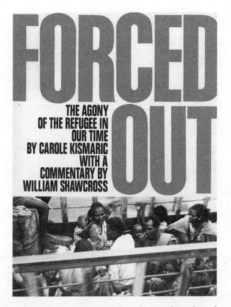

*Forced Out* was a 1989 book on the already-worldwide refugee crisis. The book was primarily funded by the J.M. Kaplan Fund.
CREDIT: CAROLE KISMARIC

fourteen million refugees in the world. Now there are over fifty million."

The large book, styled like newsprint, is filled with painful photographs of throngs crossing the desert in Africa, boat people escaping Vietnam, dead Haitians washed up on the Florida coast, Palestinian refugee camps around the Middle East, and more. First-person tales of escape and disappointment—"painful choices, terrible odds"—fill page after page. This was 1989, but refugees from some of the same countries we see today are included: Afghanistan, Iran, Iraq, Ethiopia.

"Originally, Human Rights Watch started as Helsinki Watch that was mainly concerned with dissident writers who were in trouble around the world and what could we do about protecting them," Joan said. "We and a handful of top publishers had first gotten together to support an underground paper in Europe and Russia called *Index*, and out of that group eventually came Human Rights Watch and we were the first grantors of that, I believe."

The harsh realities of the world rarely escaped Fund notice and support. Homelessness was one of those realities, starting with J.M.'s early interest in the soon to be well-known advocate Robert Hayes. As a young lawyer at the white-shoe firm of Sullivan & Cromwell, Hayes, then living on the border of Chelsea and Greenwich Village, had "encountered a number of homeless men."

"I talked with them, listened, and got to know them," he told me in a phone interview. "What I learned, basically, was there were no safe places for these homeless folks to go, and the numbers of people on the streets was increasing dramatically."

Hayes was just out of NYU Law School and had very little litigation experience, but he wanted to do something. When he met with city officials, there was no interest in helping, he recalled. He then turned to litigation, bringing a lawsuit on behalf of the homeless and arguing for their "right to shelter."

The state Supreme Court ordered the city to provide emergency shelter to homeless men, and by August 1981 Hayes had signed a consent decree with the city, making permanent the right to shelter. (Currently, more than sixty thousand New

Yorkers are sheltered each night.) He then decided to leave his law firm and, with a small group of allies, launch the Coalition for the Homeless to expand the advocacy beyond a single lawsuit. For that, charitable donations were needed.

His first stop in 1981 was Linda Gillies at the Astor Foundation, which often, like the J.M. Kaplan Fund, was an innovative, locally focused funder. Gillies then introduced him to Suzanne Davis, who brought him to J.M. "I think Suzanne liked the idea of a twentysomething Wall Street lawyer wanting to change the world," Hayes said. "[J.M.] was a crusty sort," Hayes remembered. "At one meeting we were chatting and he asked about my family. I would have told him that my father was a small businessman who died when I was twelve. My mother was a high school teacher at public schools in Queens. I told him my mom was at first appalled by my shift to starting the Coalition for the Homeless and giving up the security of a Wall Street law firm. But then she visited the coalition offices and, having retired that year as a teacher, became the volunteer bookkeeper at the coalition for the next seven years."

With support from the J.M. Kaplan Fund and others, the Coalition for the Homeless became an incessant voice for the rights of the homeless poor in the courts and in the media. In the mid-1980s, Hayes won a MacArthur "genius grant" and gave it to the coalition. He said with a laugh, "I wanted to be the largest funder." In 1989, Hayes left the coalition to return to being "a real lawyer in the New York City office of the firm headed by Warren Christopher." Hayes's work established the fundamental legal framework for the city's responsibility for the homeless.

Later, Hayes wound up handling a case in Portland, Maine, fell in love with the city, and spent the 1990s there, practicing law and raising three daughters. He returned to New York in 2002 as president of the Medicare Rights Center. Since 2015, Hayes has been the president and CEO of Community Healthcare Network, which runs fourteen health centers throughout New York City, bringing medical and behavioral health care and other social services to underserved men, women, and children.

## HELP FOR THE UNDERSERVED

Then there was the issue of public toilets. In 1990, the Legal Action Center for the Homeless filed a class-action lawsuit claiming that the failure to provide sufficient public toilet facilities constituted a public nuisance and recommended the automatic public toilets (APTs) manufactured by JCDecaux, the French company that provides them in Europe. At Joan's suggestion, the Fund wrote to JCDecaux, who agreed to demonstrate the toilets in New York if the Fund paid to install them. Suzanne Davis took on the campaign with gusto and raised $235,000 from a broad base of supporters, including $50,000 from the Fund. After a successful six-month demonstration in 1992, the program was deemed a success and the city issued a request for proposals for new street furniture, including APTs. Although NYC today has only a handful of APTs, the experiment led to a public-toilet revolution in cities across the country. Last year, JCDecaux purchased the street-furniture contract from the company that had won the bid and is now operating bus shelters, newsstands, and a handful of APTs around the city, with reported plans to install more of the public toilets in the near future.

Coincidentally, during the time of the lawsuit, Joan met with Bryant Park director Dan Biederman. He solicited money from her to restore a park statue and, instead, she offered to upgrade the tawdry public restrooms. The Fund financed the highly admired restoration of this essential public toilet on 42nd Street. The agreement provided that both restrooms would always have fresh flowers and an attendant.

Legal support for the underserved was a constant for the Fund. Observed Tony Wood: "Funders often shy away from financing legal work." It is often a bottomless pit (see Chapter 5). "But," added Wood, "J.M. realized the need for a legal stick to back up a commitment of any kind. The need was clear that the legal capacity within movements was an ongoing need. This is another example of the Kaplan Fund strategy of supporting a movement strategically in different capacities."

The Fund showed up as well with its support for legal aid on behalf of the AIDS crisis. As Wood recalled, "We chased down Tom Stoddard of the Lambda Legal Defense and Education Fund to get him to put in an application and then doubled the amount he asked for. This was an important moment in time in the gay rights movement."

Stoddard, who died in 1997 at the age of forty-eight of an AIDS-related cancer, brought the law to bear on the AIDS crisis, as Hayes had done for the homeless.[5] Stoddard had graduated NYU Law School in 1977, and after serving as counsel to Barbara Shack, the legislative director for the New

York Civil Liberties Union, he succeeded her in 1982, when the death penalty and abortion rights were at the top of the agenda. From there, he became executive director of Lambda Legal in 1986, when Wood sought him out on behalf of the Fund. The organization had initiated the fight against discrimination against gays and AIDS patients in employment, housing, and health care. Stoddard grew Lambda Legal into a nationally influential organization, with the staff increasing from six to twenty-two people.

Suzanne Davis remembers that the Fund was one of the first to support the legal efforts on behalf of the gay population. The Fund's involvement with Stoddard and especially Hayes transformed Davis from administrator and all-around helper to an out-and-out activist. "I was educated by Bob Hayes, and he sparked my interest in pursuing related causes, especially the coat drive I started in 1989," which encouraged people to donate their gently used coats to convenient collection points around the city, including major transportation hubs, police and fire stations, and libraries. "We discovered this young organization of volunteers working in Riverside Park," Davis recalled. "They seemed a perfect source of manpower to run the coat drive." Their director, Kenneth Adams, quickly signed on and worked with her to develop the drive. Within a few years, the program was running smoothly and became a signature program of New York Cares. In 2018, the thirtieth year of the coat drive, volunteers collected and distributed the two millionth coat. In that year as well, Davis and the Fund were honored at the New York Cares Gala for this early leadership and advocacy on behalf of homeless New Yorkers.

## BOOKS, BOOKS, AND MORE BOOKS

Free expression and books are another theme appearing in all of Joan's, the family's, and the Fund's work. Joan loves books. She loves to read them, help get them published, and make sure they are designed well. Her residences in Manhattan and the Hudson Valley are filled with books—on tables and in well-lit wall shelves. Many of the books were funded by either the Fund or her own Furthermore program. Furthermore alone has helped publish over one thousand books. Her superb publication on the refugee crises, *Forced Out*, was a collaboration with Human Rights Watch. Four major publishers came together to print and distribute it. Joan is also a good writer and editor, having produced hundreds of speeches, forewords and introductions to books on a wide range of subjects, letters

Poets House—a library, literary center, and event space in Battery Park City overlooking the Hudson—was a favorite cause of Mary Kaplan.
CREDIT: ELIZABETH FELICELLA

to the editor, and essays. More often than not, the books and her writing reflect many of the issues presented in this book.

All the Kaplans have a history with some form of the printed word. Books are a thick thread in the Fund's history. Mary Kaplan, Joan's sister, loved to support the publication of books and journals, as well as the organizations that nurture writers—be they poets, authors, or broadcasters.

Mary, in fact, helped found Poets House, a national poetry library and literary center, in 1985 with Stanley Kunitz, two-time poet laureate of the United States. Mary also funded *Partisan Review* for many years.

Writer and City College English professor Mark Mirsky, a founder of *Fiction* magazine, told me in an interview, "Without Mary, the magazine would have collapsed."[6] The founders didn't ask her for money, but she heard through a friend that the magazine was in trouble and, Mirsky recalled, "asked, 'Do you need help?' She was our advocate." Mirsky eventually became a close friend of Mary's. "She was agile and funny and had a coterie of literary friends. She loves books and the theater. My book on Shakespeare is dedicated to her because she kept sweeping me along with her to watch his plays in performance." Mirsky observed, "She favored personal giving, helping people directly, not giving to institutions."

Elizabeth Kaplan Fonseca, another Kaplan sister, helped rescue the Mount, legendary writer Edith Wharton's house in Lenox, Massachusetts, when it was facing foreclosure and bank sale. Wharton—who, in addition to penning numerous novels and short stories, wrote about her own ideas about good architecture—designed the house in 1902. It is an elegant,

IN SPITE OF ILLNESS, IN SPITE
EVEN OF THE ARCHENEMY
SORROW, ONE CAN REMAIN
ALIVE LONG PAST THE USUAL
DATE OF DISINTEGRATION IF
ONE IS UNAFRAID OF CHANGE,
INSATIABLE IN INTELLECTUAL
CURIOSITY, INTERESTED
IN BIG THINGS, AND
HAPPY IN SMALL WAYS.

—EDITH WHARTON

In Memory of Alice M. Kaplan

Generous donations directed by Elizabeth Kaplan Fonseca made possible the successful campaign to save the 1902 Mount, designed and built by Edith Wharton. At the time, it was facing possible foreclosure.
CREDIT: THE MOUNT, EDITH WHARTON'S HOME

four-story, white stucco house, topped with clusters of gables and chimneys and surrounded by accessory buildings, formal gardens, and mature woodlands. She built it with royalties from her books and lived there with her husband until 1911.

The Mount's executive director, Susan Wissler, explained that Elizabeth "was appalled to learn from her doctor, Elizabeth Beautyman, whose husband, Gordon Travis, was on the board, that the Mount was over $8 million in debt and due to be foreclosed and sold." In 2009, using her share of the proceeds of a sale of a valuable painting that had belonged to her mother, Alice, Elizabeth donated $800,000. This pivotal gift provided the institution with the means and the time to restructure its bank debt and mount a major fundraising campaign. "Betty's gift marked the beginning of the transformation of the Mount into both an important tourist site and a year-round cultural center that today hosts a steady roster of programs in partnership with over forty other cultural and social organizations." This grant is also indicative of the different style of giving that Elizabeth favored. Whereas Joan championed small grants to many entities, Elizabeth believed in more comprehensive, and fewer, large-scale grants.

A modest marble plaque, dedicated to Alice Kaplan, rests along a garden wall with a quotation from a Wharton novel. Elizabeth was already a Wharton fan and had posted this quote in her kitchen: "In spite of illness, in spite even of the archenemy sorrow, one *can* remain alive long past the usual date of disintegration if one is unafraid of change, insatiable in intellectual curiosity, interested in big things, and happy in small ways."[7]

Just as the J.M. Kaplan Fund and later Joan's own Furthermore program have funded the new, the obscure, the bold, or the adventurous in all manner of fields, the Fund supported books that didn't just complement those efforts but that found a way to advance a new cause or fill a vacuum in the publishing world at the time. As Joan has worn many hats over the years—including head of the New York State Council on the Arts and the New York State Office for Parks, Recreation, and Historic Preservation—books have always fallen within the same spheres of interest as her activities. When Joan gave up her stewardship of the Fund in 1993 to head New York State parks, books continued to gain Fund support and, at Joan's behest, state funding as well. When Joan left that appointed post and the Fund continued under the leadership of the next Kaplan generation, she established the new Fund program, Furthermore, focused exclusively on supporting nonfiction publishing in her selected fields: art, architecture, and design; cultural history; preservation; and the environment.[8]

Fund books often reflected the new or nascent causes that the Fund clearly intended to bring attention to. With the NRDC, Joan published a number of books warning about the dangers of atomic energy. With the Consumers Union, she published *Below the Line: Living Poor in America*. She supported the New York Public Library's catalog of censored books and PEN America's effort to defend imprisoned freedom-of-conscience writers. There was the helpful *Juror's Guide to Lower Manhattan*, to educate and entertain jurors on their lunch hour, that the Municipal Art Society published.

The *Design Guide for Rural Roads* was published by the Dutchess Land Conservancy in 1988 with grant support from both the Rural New York program and Furthermore (as well as others). Even the esoteric was embraced and supported, such as the South Street Seaport's catalog from the Herman Melville Library on shipbuilding, whaling, and maritime law.

Joan's awareness of the importance and power of words extended, as well, to the radio, resulting in a significant impact on the Albany-based National Public Radio (NPR) station, WAMC Northeast Public Radio. On her own initiative, she became a crucial donor at just the right time. Alan Chartock, the president and CEO of WAMC and a professor emeritus at the University at Albany, had built this NPR affiliate from a scrappy local station run by him and a bunch of college interns into a formidable force reaching six northeastern states.[9] Raising money in bits and pieces, mostly through on-air appeals, was barely keeping the station going when Joan unexpectedly appeared on the scene.

Chartock told me in an interview: "I was sitting in my office when this woman walks in. I don't know who she is, and she is accompanied by a staff person, Tony Wood. She introduces herself and I don't even know enough to stand up. She says she wants to give us money. 'My father would have wanted to support news about local government.' I said that is not what we need but what we need is funding for an environment show. At first she says, 'I don't think that's exactly what we have in mind,' but Tony interjected, 'Actually Joan, that would be great,' and she then agreed." She gave them $50,000 and continued as a regular donor personally after she resigned from the Fund. "We never had money before that," Chartock emphasized. "It had a huge impact."

That was 1998, when interest in environmental issues was emerging in a new way. *The Environment Show* was hosted by the late celebrated conservationist Peter A.A. Berle, a lawyer who served in the New York State Assembly, as president of the National Audubon Society, and as commissioner of environmental conservation. The show ran for four years and was picked up by public radio stations across the country. "She's strong and tough," Chartock said of Joan. "Don't push her around. She will make up her own mind."

Tony Wood didn't remember turning Joan around on this issue, although she put great stock in his views, but he did remember the incident. "Joan was always open to hearing what a potential grantee thought was needed, and if it made sense, would go with it—even if we originally came into the conversation with a slightly different idea," Wood said. "Joan and I did have talks about need to get our issues before the general public and how to get the work of our grantees into the popular press. Just like we felt we needed access to good lawyers, so the Fund invested in that, we knew we needed access to the press, so we explored ways to achieve that as well. It was sort of systems thinking."

## FILLING A NEED

Perhaps the most significant and successful book-related effort of the Fund was an idea of Joan's that was not about publishing books, but about selling them. It was called Urban Center

Urban Center Books, Joan's idea for a bookstore at the headquarters of MAS, carried every imaginable book related to urban and rural development.

Books, a bookstore that was part of the Municipal Art Society, located at the time in the landmark Villard Houses, designed in 1883 by McKim, Mead & White, on Madison Avenue and 50th Street. In 1980, after a long civic battle over the fate of this landmark, real estate developer Harry Helmsley built a fifty-one-story hotel behind the mansion, incorporating both the center part of the U-shaped structure and the south wing into the hotel. MAS occupied the north wing on a favorably negotiated lease, with a bookstore and exhibition and meeting space on the first floor. This bookstore carried what seemed to be every book imaginable on architecture (both buildings and landscapes), urbanism, design, and housing, as well as design magazines. Both the on-site programming run by MAS and the bookstore run by John Frazier were valuable to the process of civic discourse, the involvement of far-flung communities around the city, and the advancement of needed public debate.

Their creation was somewhat serendipitous. For years, MAS, the city's primary civic voice on land-use matters, was housed in an attic office on East 65th Street belonging to the American Federation of Arts, of which Alice Kaplan was chair. Then it moved to an office at Rockefeller Center (forty-fifth floor, for a below-market rent). MAS was already mounting aggressive campaigns and acting as a formidable civic voice. Then came the Grand Central fight. As part of the campaign to save Grand Central Terminal (Chapter 4), MAS opened a storefront near the station, primarily funded by Joan. "People came in and out all day," recalled then MAS executive director Margot Welling-ton. "We had a few things for sale like ties and buttons—'No more bites out of the Big Apple'—and a few books."

The storefront gave the organization a new perspective on the public for whom they were advocating, and the public got to know about MAS. "The presence on the street was so very important," recalled Joan. The late Fred Papert, an MAS board member, had commented on how nice it would be if the orga-nization had a permanent street presence in its own building, the kind they had had for the Grand Central fight. As exec-utive director, Wellington was authorized to look "for a small building in Midtown that we could buy," she recalled in an interview. "That was when Midtown was still filled with small buildings that you could buy for $650,000." She was actively looking when she was alerted by architectural historian Bill Shopsin that developer Harry Helmsley did not know what to do with the north wing of the Villard Houses. MAS had led a contentious and successful campaign to save that building, causing Helmsley to incorporate the landmark into his new hotel.[10] The former home of Random House, the north wing now had a wrecked interior, but it was an appropriate place for MAS. "It had cubicles, dropped ceilings, and peeling paint," Wellington said. But she knew it was just right for creating a home for MAS, a gathering place called the Urban Center, and an informal crossroads for people involved or just interested in city development issues. Wellington started bringing potential donors through the building, including Joan.

Wellington remembered it vividly: "Joan stood in the lobby, looked around, and asked, 'Have you thought about having a bookstore?' We hadn't, of course, but I said maybe in the future. Then she asked, 'Where would you put it and what would it look like?' and we both looked at that room facing the courtyard and said that would be perfect." And so it happened, with Fund support. But this was not any ordinary bookstore.

"It was a great place to bump into other architects," architect Robert A.M. Stern told me in an interview. "It was also a great resource to discover new publications." The Urban Center itself, Stern added, was important as a place where "the network of groups" was housed, so the interaction among them—MAS, the Architectural League of New York, the Parks Council, AIA New York—was very beneficial. "A lost culture," as Stern described it. "It made all of us so much stronger than any of us had ever been," said Wellington.

While Wellington was meeting with Joan, the legendary *New Yorker* writer, indefatigable preservationist, and MAS board member Brendan Gill was persuading Brooke Astor to support MAS's move to create the Urban Center. Mrs. Astor was not an early and eager preservationist, but Gill won her over, and she generously supported the Urban Center. Later, she would join the fight to stop Saint Bartholomew's Church from selling off its community house and join the Fund in the effort to stop developer Peter Kalikow from demolishing blocks built by City and Suburban Homes on the Upper East Side (Chapter 4).

Urban Center Books and the Urban Center itself became a must-see stop for every out-of-town visitor interested in subjects about the built city, foreign or domestic, and, in the process, the center became a highly valued meeting place for serendipitous encounters. "We had a visitor from Venezuela who came with an empty suitcase to fill with books whenever he came to New York," Wellington recalled. "There weren't many places with our kind of selection." Of course, this was before Amazon, but, as one observer noted, "replacing the brick with the click is sad."

The Urban Center opened in 1980 with two exhibits "that projected dueling visions of the brick and mortar future of the city," as A.G. Sulzberger describes in the *New York Times*.[11] "In one, an elaborate plastic model of Grand Central Terminal was designed to crumble to pieces repeatedly. The other celebrated six prominent planned additions to the New York City skyline, including what became the Jacob K. Javits Convention Center."

"Most of the great campaigns, whether it was preserving a landmark, protecting the waterfront, fighting the height of the new Columbus Circle tower, saving a park, or supporting affordable housing, it all happened in this building," former MAS president Kent Barwick told me in an interview.

The Urban Center served, in effect, as a civic commons. The ground floor was the most important space in the building, with its exhibits, lectures, design presentations, and panel discussions. It played a role that is sorely missed today, and it attracted fifty thousand visitors a year.[12] The bookstore, the only one of its kind in the city, was across from two spacious and elegant rooms where the exhibitions and forums—and sometimes

A panel discussion was held at MAS headquarters in 1990 on the future of the Penn Yards site, now Hudson Yards. L to R: Richard Sennett, then NYU professor of sociology; Edmund N. Bacon, former executive director of Philadelphia City Planning Commission; Brendan Gill, longtime contributor to the *New Yorker*; and the author, Roberta Brandes Gratz.
CREDIT: DOROTHY ALEXANDER

heated debates—on critical city issues took place. There was great synergy; one might come to buy a book and discover an illuminating exhibit on proposed new zoning policies, or hear a lecture advocating more transit options and proposals to limit car traffic. An exhibit on the community's alternative proposal to the Clinton Hill neighborhood urban-renewal plan, for example, helped local activists negotiate a better plan with the city and avoid some unnecessary demolition and relocation. The Fund supported the publication of an accompanying catalog of that exhibit. Other neighborhood plans had similar effects. Authors often held book publication parties at the Urban Center. Unplanned encounters often led to new initiatives.

When the Urban Center was at its peak, the exhibits highlighted the advocacy campaign of the moment—Saint Bart's, for example, or a proposed Fifth Avenue historic district—and the lectures, programs, and tours were aligned with that same advocacy topic. Every public-education tool was focused on the current MAS agenda, and the Urban Center and bookstore were the ultimate toolbox. It was a Madison Avenue showcase for topics from all over the city, giving real visibility and prominence to causes in all the boroughs that otherwise might never have been seen by the larger public.

Out of the creation of the Urban Center came another brilliant idea of great civic importance, Wellington pointed out, this one thought of by MAS board member Doris C. Freedman.[13] First organized around her dining room table and then monthly at the Urban Center, a gathering of the presidents of twelve urban-development-related organizations met monthly, forming the Presidents' Council. "Nobody was allowed to substitute for the organization president at the meetings," Wellington said. "All would present ideas and issues of current importance and often organized as a single voice, creating a formidable show of civic force." Some observers criticized the idea of a single voice, noting that it muted the multiple perspectives that needed to be heard. Nevertheless, the voice of the President's Council was powerful.

Founded in 1893, MAS was for more than one hundred years a strong advocate for livable-city initiatives in a wide-ranging number of fields. Its advocacy, while selective, was often courageous in the face of pressures from real estate interests or city hall. The board, a committee of respected professionals and activists, helped the staff decide what to testify on at the City Planning Commission, the Landmarks Preservation Commission, the Art Commission, and the Board of Standards and Appeals. Joan was a long-term board member, strong voice, and key funder. Before the leadership change in 2010, MAS had taken a generous buyout of its lease from the Helmsley organization, with the expectation of finding a new street-level location. The calculus was that the lease buyout would provide the core funding for a permanent home, and several donors had made major pledges to add to it.

Urban Center Books closed in 2010 but was expected to be part of a new location. None of that happened. Instead, under new leadership, MAS moved back to upstairs offices, first on West 57th Street and then on Madison Avenue and 51st Street on the nineteenth floor. In the process, the idea of on-the-ground civic connections, high-impact advocacy, and a street-level site for meaningful civic engagement was lost, as was Urban Center Books. Joan tried in vain to find another location for the bookstore, but nothing seemed to work.

Joan's belief in and commitment to the Municipal Art Society was huge, but she took as much pleasure in some of the smallest projects of her own, representing something new and unique. Often, she funded them herself. In 1978, she worked with nonprofit publisher and old friend Mike Gladstone to produce a series of artists' postcards that "explored the postcard as an art form as well as an ancient tool of communication." This project reflected her attention to detail, no matter how small, and her commitment to the arts of all kinds. They were high-quality, general-circulation postcards made from original artworks created expressly for the postcard and made to postcard scale. Gladstone—the editor, publisher, and designer for the project—had been head of publications for MoMA, among other institutions. Both known and unknown artists were selected, some of whom were not yet widely recognized but would become so. Artists included Robert Mapplethorpe, David Hockney, Massimo Vignelli, Hugh Kepets, and Alex Katz. Poetry and cityscape photographs were included as well. They had "much fun" with this project, Joan recalled.

## THINKING SMALL IN A BIG WAY

It may seem strange to talk about the coat drive—the inventive, popular happening organized by Suzanne Davis—in the same breath as Human Rights Watch. Or to talk about the vest-pocket parks at the same time as the Herculean, long-term effort to restore Central Park, or the serendipitous beginning of the High Line. And maybe the fight against Robert Moses to save Washington Square Park doesn't seem nearly as significant as the gradual upstate property acquisition to save the New York City watershed. Or even the fights to save Ladies' Mile or SoHo might pale in comparison to the significance of the battles to save Grand Central and Saint Bartholomew's Church. The big ones, and the ones that may have been small to start but large to finish, are the ones that sometimes get noticed in the press; the little ones, the seeds, not so much. However, many of these more modest efforts inspired other small efforts that spread over the whole city and, collectively, had a huge impact. In many cases, they proliferated around the state and beyond. In every corner of the city where Robert Moses's urban renewal, slum clearance, or highway projects could be found, neighborhoods were disrupted or destroyed. The efforts described here all sought to repair the damage or humanize the newly built projects.

Yet, the idea still prevails, as it did in the '70s, that these micro efforts are too small, too ad hoc, not big in impact or import. Hopefully, instead, one can recognize here the enormous collective value of the many disparate ways the J.M. Kaplan Fund supported innovative ideas, regardless of scale, thought up by active citizens—citizens wanting in some small way to repair their neighborhood or their city and collectively accomplishing just that.

Over the past fifty years in New York City and State, many, many more efforts have evolved that were not funded by—or probably not even known to—J.M., Joan, and the alert and energetic staff of the J.M. Kaplan Fund. It is a local and national imperative, however, that all such efforts be encouraged and nourished, even if they only last long enough to have a modest impact or to sprout new efforts. Especially now, in the age of big-checkbook philanthropy directing megabucks at big problems, there is still a need and a place for the likes of the Fund, strategically deploying modest grants to passionate individuals creatively tackling the problems around them. The lessons of the Fund can be applied by any philanthropist, great or small, and now, thanks to online giving platforms, it is easier than ever for everyone, at some level, to be a philanthropist. More than ever, we need the Kaplan brand of philanthropy.

While the Fund under J.M. Kaplan and his offspring, most significantly Joan, has helped change the history of New York City and State in the many ways demonstrated here, the next generation continues the tradition, but now sets their sights beyond the horizon of New York.

As Joan observed: "The next generation is carrying on, honoring the traditions and the practices of their forebears and charting new directions as well. And the generation after that, waiting in the wings, is already champing at the bit, to take the work farther still in their turn." It is a formidable legacy to build on.

The Kaplan family
CREDIT: THE J.M. KAPLAN FUND

# ACKNOWLEDGMENTS

Author's Note: I first met Joan K. Davidson in the early 1970s when I was a reporter for the *New York Post* under Dorothy Schiff. I was covering many of the stories included in this book. That is when I first witnessed the impact of Joan and the J.M. Kaplan Fund as a force for positive change. After leaving the newspaper, I wrote three books that covered some of the challenges, controversies, and distinct periods of urban change, particularly in New York City, described herein. References to those prior books are included. A few years ago, I and a number of Joan's friends discussed the challenge of making the public aware of Joan's legacy and her impact, especially on some of the most vexing and controversial issues of recent decades. My reaction was: "There needs to be a book." And so here it is.

First of all, this book represents hours and hours of conversation with Joan, during which we both relished revisiting the victories and defeats experienced by the city over the past several decades. This book, however, could not have been written without the enormous help and great memory of Tony Wood, a former Fund staff member and close friend of Joan's. Kent Barwick, who has been a friend and colleague of Joan's for decades, was also critical, as was Suzanne Davis, who worked at the Fund over many years. Amy L. Freitag, current J.M. Kaplan Fund executive director; Liz Meshel, program and grants assistant; William P. Falahee, director of finance and administration; and Ann Birckmayer, administrator of Furthermore, were all tremendously helpful. I am grateful to Mary Beth Betts for her image research. For a while, Daniel Lo-Preto served as my editor in the early stages of this book and until he went on to bigger things. Appreciation goes to Katy O'Donnell, Michelle Welsh-Horst, and Elizabeth Dana for bringing it across the finish line.

The following people were also helpful, in interviews or in remembering things that happened or both: John Adams, Wint Aldrich, Laurie Beckelman, Carmi Bee, Marcy Benstock, Mitch Bernard, Peter Brink, Al Butzel, Alan Chartock, Brad Davidson, Betsy Davidson, Matthew Davidson, Peter W. Davidson, Gordon Davis, Henry Ng, Mark Mirsky, Andrew Dolkart, Isabel Fonseca, Richard George, Linda Gillies, Stephen A. Goldsmith, Eric Goldstein, Robert Hayes, Clay Hiles, Alexia Lalli, Richard Meier, Aryeh Neier, Elizabeth Barlow Rogers, David Sampson, Isaac Stern, Robert A.M. Stern, Tania Werbizky, Margot Wellington, Susan Wissler, and Robert Yaro.

# NOTES

## Preface: Moving Forward

1. In 2019, the Fund was worth $143 million.

## Chapter 1: Practice, Practice, Practice

1. That name didn't last. It was renamed Avery Fisher Hall in 1973 and then David Geffen Hall in 2015. The Metropolitan Opera retained its name when it, too, moved to Lincoln Center. The incomparable, acoustically famous 1883 "old Met" was demolished in January 1967, despite the public pleading of famed orchestra leader Leopold Stokowski. The Landmarks Preservation Commission, not yet two years old, voted six to five not to designate it, thus sealing its fate.

2. Stern lived from 1920 to 2001. John P. Callahan, "Red Tower Is Set for Carnegie Site," *New York Times*, August 8, 1957.

3. See Robert A. Caro's *The Power Broker: Robert Moses and the Fall of New York* (New York: Knopf, 1974), for a brilliant history of Moses' influence and impact.

4. The current leadership is the third generation Kaplans.

5. In 1949, President Harry Truman signed the Housing Act, which gave federal, state, and local governments unprecedented power to shape residential life. One of the Housing Act's main initiatives—urban renewal—destroyed about two thousand communities in the 1950s and '60s and forced more than three hundred

thousand families from their homes. Overall, about half of urban renewal's victims were black, a reality that led to James Baldwin's famous quip that "urban renewal means Negro removal." Kwame Shakir, "Gentrification Is 'Negro Removal': A Parasitically Vicious Attack Against POC Communities," AFROPUNK, March 6, 2018, https://afropunk.com/2018/03/gentrification-negro-removal-para sitically-vicious-attack-poc-communities/.

6. Caro, *Power Broker*, 12.

7. Jane Jacobs's *Death and Life of Great American Cities* (New York: Random House, 1961), challenged that view and began to change the way the world views cities.

8. Similar diminishment of federally built public housing has been happening since the Reagan administration, and nonstop through every administration since. See Roberta Brandes Gratz, "Public Housing and Disaster Capitalism," in *We're Still Here Ya Bastards: How the People of New Orleans Rebuilt Their City* (New York: Bold Type Books, 2015), 277–298.

9. Caro, *Power Broker*, 20.

10. A major urban renewal site on the Lower East Side of Manhattan, for example, Essex Crossing has just been built in 2020, filling the void left by urban renewal demolition fifty years ago. The site has remained a series of empty blocks since then.

11. Clyde Haberman, "Movies Can Take New Yorkers Back to the '70s. But Why Go There?," *New York Times*, July 4, 2017, www .nytimes.com/2017/07/04/opinion/nyc-1970s-mta-subways.html.

12. Caro, *Power Broker*, 20.

13. Until World War II, cities developed naturally with businesses, residences, institutions and other uses cheek by jowl with one another. New planning and zoning thinking called for a "separation" of all those naturally integrated uses.

14. The New York Coliseum complex at Columbus Circle, Lincoln Towers, and the West Side Urban Renewal project, among others.

15. Ground was broken in 1959. The first building, Philharmonic Hall, opened in 1962.

16. Michael Cooper, "A Starburst Is Born: Watch the Building of the Metropolitan Opera," *New York Times*, September 15, 2017.

17. In June 2016, Lincoln Center released a report outlining its economic contributions to NYC as a cultural destination, big employer, and tourist attraction. It was preparing to ask the city to contribute public funds to the newest makeover of Philharmonic Hall, now called David Geffen Hall. It reported 4,547 employees and 4.5 million attendees, a third of whom attended free events. Non–New Yorkers, who cited Lincoln Center as a "very important reason" for their trips, spent $669 million elsewhere in the city. Michael Cooper, "Lincoln Center Report: We Entertain, Educate, Accept Tax Dollars," *New York Times*, June 13, 2016.

18. For example, my husband and I bought a West 87th Street brownstone with no thought of Lincoln Center but, instead, thinking of having a house so we could stay in the city and not move to a suburb.

19. See Mindy Thompson Fullilove's *Root Shock: How Tearing Up City Neighborhoods Hurts America, and What We Can Do About It* (Oakland, CA: New Village Press, 2016) for an understanding of how displacement undermines families and the larger social order.

20. Roberta Brandes Gratz, *The Living City: How America's Cities Are Being Revitalized by Thinking Small in a Big Way* (Hoboken, NJ: Wiley, 1994), 312.

21. Roberta Brandes Gratz, *The Battle for Gotham: New York in the Shadow of Robert Moses and Jane Jacobs* (New York: Nation Books, 2010), 131. Adding up many of the neighborhoods bulldozed, I estimated about one million residents were displaced—and that does not count businesses, factories, schools, and institutions.

22. She loved playing four-handed piano.

23. In 1986, Carnegie Hall reopened after a three-year renovation led by architect James Polshek. An exhibit about the massive job and fundraising effort gave short shrift to the earlier work by Isaac Stern and J.M. Kaplan to save the building from demolition. I volunteered to Joan to interview Stern on tape for Fund archives. All comments by Stern here are from that taped interview.

24. Lisa Greenwald, "History of the J.M. Kaplan Fund" (submitted to the trustees May 2004), 5.

25. Dean Rusk was president of the Rockefeller Foundation from 1952 to 1960.

26. The Damrosch family was a New York family including several musicians. Damrosch Park at Lincoln Center is named after them.

27. "Farewell to Penn Station," *New York Times*, October 30, 1963. Related reading: Ada Louise Huxtable, "Architecture: How to Kill a City," *New York Times*, May 5, 1963.

28. Although some Moses defenders claim this is not true, Robert Caro documents this well: "He loves the public, but not as people. . . . He began taking measures to limit use of his parks. He had restricted use of state parks by poor and lower-middle-class families. . . . He vetoed the Long Island Rail Road's proposed branch spur to Jones Beach. . . . He instructed Shapiro to build the bridges across his new parkways low—too low for buses to pass. . . . Buses chartered by Negro groups found it very difficult to obtain permits." (Caro, *Power Broker*, 318). In my own research for *The Battle for Gotham*, I called the state's transportation department. I was told that some of the bridges have since been rebuilt higher, but that large vehicles can hardly fit under most of the old bridges, except in the absolute middle.

29. Caro, *Power Broker*, 20.

30. The new Catholic chapel is visible through the Washington Square Arch when coming down Fifth Avenue.

31. Anthony C. Wood, *Preserving New York: Winning the Right to Protect a City's Landmarks* (New York: Routledge, 2007), 182.

32. Eleanor Roosevelt had an apartment at 29 Washington Square West, overlooking the park.

33. Wood, *Preserving New York*, 189.

34. Gratz, *The Battle for Gotham*, 76.

35. No one studied the question "Where did the traffic go?" which prompted Jacobs to comment to me that transportation planners are never curious enough to explore this phenomenon after roads are removed.

36. Robert Moses's Cadman Plaza/BQE plan would have demolished at least ninety buildings in Brooklyn Heights, but after years of fighting by the Brooklyn Heights Association, demolition was contained and the BQE was placed under the esplanade.

37. Alan Burnham eventually published the list in his book *New York Landmarks* (Middletown, CT: Wesleyan Press, 1963). But it was in process starting in the 1950s.

38. The Central Park defeat was one of Moses's earliest losses—as Robert Caro shows in *The Power Broker*—not the proposed road through Washington Square, as is often mistakenly claimed.

39. This is still true. In many cases, the city is a poor steward of its own landmark buildings, leaving them exposed to the elements to fall further into decay so that their deteriorated condition becomes the excuse to tear them down when convenient, as happened in recent years at the Brooklyn Navy Yard.

40. Since the early 2000s, the Landmarks Preservation Commission has been reluctant to designate interiors.

## Chapter 2: The Founder

1. "A Message from J.M. Kaplan," Fall 1956. This message was in response to a tribute from the National Grape Co-operative Association, Inc., representing some 4,500 grape growers, after the September 1, 1956, transfer to the grape growers of the international business, with its annual sales volume of $40 million.

2. Greenwald, "J.M. Kaplan Fund," 6.

3. Interview with Lisa Greenwald, November 20, 2014.

4. A catalog of her collection was published in 1981.

## Chapter 3: Sound the Trumpets

1. Andrew Dolkart wrote a brilliant, fascinating, and detailed report for the National Register of Historic Places to secure federal landmark status for Westbeth. His report was of great help for the

story here. Dolkart says there are five buildings but, "with all the additions . . . you can count buildings in different ways." Department of the Interior, National Register of Historic Places Registration Form, "Westbeth" (prepared by Andrew S. Dolkart and Greenwich Village Society for Historic Preservation), www.gvshp.org/_gvshp /preservation/fwv/doc/westbeth-nrn.pdf.

2. Dolkart notes that the first neighborhood Halloween parade— which has become such a huge tradition—was organized and started here. "Westbeth," section 8, p. 11.

3. Richard Kaplan, interview by Liz McEnaney, October 19, 2014, at request of the Fund.

4. Roberta Brandes Gratz with Norman Mintz, "The Soho Syndrome," in *Cities Back From the Edge: New Life for Downtown* (Hoboken, NJ: Wiley, 1998), 295.

5. A study by planner Chester Rapkin in 1963 discovered fifty categories of industrial activity still in the district. Gratz and Mintz, "Soho Syndrome," 296.

6. Grace Glueck, "Co-op in 'Village' to House Artists," *New York Times*, April 8, 1967.

7. Thomas W. Ennis, "Bowery Hotel Where Derelicts Slept Being Converted to Artist Studios," *New York Times*, August 6, 1967.

8. Joan Davidson, interview by Jeanne Houck, March 13, 2007, transcript, Oral History Collection—Westbeth, Greenwich Village Society for Historic Preservation, New York.

9. The unused rail line was subsequently supported over many years by the Fund, first as a restored railway and then as the High Line.

10. Davidson, interview by Houck, 13.

11. Richard developed his own practice, worked on the team that designed the award-winning Chatham Towers in Lower Manhattan, and was most proud of a unique private home he designed on a hilltop overlooking the ocean in Montauk, Long Island.

12. Breuer's famous Whitney Museum on Madison Avenue, opened in 1966, was taken over by the Metropolitan Museum of Art when the Whitney opened its new quarters on the Lower West Side in 2015 designed by Renzo Piano.

13. The American Federation of Arts is a nonprofit organization that organizes art exhibitions for presentation in museums around the world, publishes exhibition catalogs, and develops education programs.

14. Dolkart, "Westbeth," section 8, p. 9.

15. Ada Louise Huxtable, "Architecture," *New York Times*, May 10, 1970.

16. Goldsmith went on to be the first artist in the country appointed to run a city planning commission, appointed by then mayor Ross "Rocky" Anderson, subsequently taught urban planning at the University of Utah, and is now executive director of the Center for the Living City, of which I am president.

17. It was listed on the National Register of Historic Places. It was designated a local landmark by the NYC Landmarks Preservation Commission in 2016.

18. Westbeth has both a board of directors, made up of nonresidents, to assure that new tenants qualify as artists and the Artists Residents Council, which runs the building.

19. Today, Joan said, how to keep it a place for artists remains a compelling, intractable challenge.

## Chapter 4: No More Bites

1. John Kenneth Galbraith, "The Economic and Social Returns of Preservation," in *Preservation: Toward an Ethic in the 1980s*, ed. National Trust for Historic Preservation (Washington, DC: Preservation Press, 1980), 57.

2. *The Living City*, my first book, documents this period. Urban renewal, in all its forms, was slowing down but not ending. Looking at pictures of dense, mixed-income neighborhoods condemned and destroyed in the name of slum clearance can make one weep. Blocks and blocks of tightly placed, solid structures densely built would be high-priced targets for renovation today.

3. Gratz, *The Living City*, 11.

4. One postwar rationale for this was security. Concerns about the threat of bombs resulted in policies that included building bomb shelters.

5. Ada Louise Huxtable, "Architectural View," *New York Times*, May 30, 1976.

6. Others included the Mertz Gilmore Foundation, the Vincent Astor Foundation, and, later, the Warhol Foundation for the Visual Arts.

7. Other collaborators included the Robert Sterling Clark Foundation, New York Community Trust, J.P. Morgan, Surdna Foundation, Scherman Foundation, Rockefeller Brothers Fund, and Mertz Charitable Trust.

8. If the owner could show he was not earning a 6 percent return on his investment, he could apply for de-landmarking and demolish the structure.

9. When I started writing about historic preservation for the *New York Post* in 1970, many people told me Brendan Gill was the most important person to talk to. I did, and he encouraged me to stick with it.

10. Paul Goldberger succeeded Gill.

11. NY Preservation Archive Project newsletter.

12. Gregory Gilmartin, *Shaping the City: New York and the Municipal Art Society*, (New York: Clarkson Potter, 1995), 405.

13. The Fund didn't do reports like this before Joan became president in 1977.

14. See Gratz, *The Living City*, for the full story of the resurrection of the South Bronx by its own residents.

15. The Real Estate Board of New York always claims the number is 19 percent, but that is Manhattan—always their chief concern.

16. Landmark designation is for the exterior of a religious building and does not interfere with religious observance.

17. This is a project for which I was a founder, and the J.M. Kaplan Fund and Vincent Astor Foundation were our first supporters.

## Chapter 5: Avoiding Armageddon

1. Joseph P. Fried, "Judge Thomas P. Griesa, Who Ruled Against Westway, Dies at 87," *New York Times*, December 26, 2017.

2. There were two rounds of Clean Water Act litigation where the case was won (in each, the courts invalidated the requisite landfill permit for the highway). In the first, resolved after two trials in 1982, Butzel was the lead lawyer and Mitch Bernard was his junior person. The second, in 1985, led to the trade-in, and Bernard was the lead lawyer with Butzel an adviser when needed.

3. Roberta Brandes Gratz, "How Westway Will Destroy New York: An Interview with Jane Jacobs," *New York Magazine*, June 1978. Gratz, *Battle for Gotham*.

4. Adam Nagourney, "A Ghost of Westway Rises Along the Hudson: An Old Idea for the Waterfront, Pared Down, Still Provokes Passions," *New York Times*, March 3, 2002.

5. Caro, *Power Broker*, 392.

6. Caro, *Power Broker*, 392.

7. Thirty years later, the challenges seem to be repeating themselves.

8. The Federal Highway Act allowed a community to trade in its highway funds for mass transit.

9. Not even mentioned here is the effect the on- and off-ramps would have on West Side neighborhoods.

10. Roberta Brandes Gratz, "The Past Over and Over Again," in *The Living City: How America's Cities Are Being Revitalized by Thinking Small in a Big Way* (Hoboken, NJ: Wiley, 1994), 339.

11. Anthony Hiss, "II—Experiencing Places," *New Yorker*, June 22, 1987.

12. The first provision of the law's general purpose states: "To preserve, protect and promote the character of the special theater district area as the location of the world's foremost concentration of legitimate theaters—an attraction which helps the City of New York achieve pre-eminent status as a cultural showcase, an office headquarters center and a cosmopolitan residential community." Gratz, *The Living City*, 341.

13. Gratz, *The Living City*, 341.

14. More theaters were here than on any other street.

15. Ada Louise Huxtable of the *New York Times* initially criticized Portman's work as "flashy, corned-up and badly detailed." Later she

recanted, heralding the architect as "a twentieth-century phenomenon" and praising his "bravura" and "extreme sensitivity to the human passages of urban design." Joyce Leviton, *People*, August 11, 1975. Quoted in Christopher Hawthorne, "Ada Louise Huxtable Memorial Explores Architecture Critic's Legacy," *Los Angeles Times*, June 5, 2013. Ada Louise Huxtable, "Design: Play It Sadly, on the Violin," *New York Times*, April 27, 1975.

16. Gratz, "The Past Over and Over Again," in *The Living City*, 337.

17. It took me a while, after hearing from so many theater people, to learn that the Morosco was the more important theatrically, if not one of the most important on Broadway, although it was understated and elegant architecturally.

18. A wide range of programs, including energy efficiency, climate change mitigation, low-income housing, access to healthy food, and more.

19. I rode with Celeste Holme, among others.

20. Under US environmental law, an environmental impact statement is a document required by the National Environmental Policy Act for certain actions "significantly affecting the quality of the human environment."

21. As had been done by architect Lewis Davis for Radio City Music Hall a year earlier, when Rockefeller Center was actually considering demolishing that iconic art deco theater.

22. This air-rights-transfer system reached the ultimate ludicrous level recently at 207 Park Avenue. Under the 2018 East Midtown zoning program, landmarks within the seventy-eight-block area can sell their air rights within the new district. So, JPMorgan Chase bought air rights from Saint Patrick's Cathedral to allow a new 1,200 feet (seventy stories) to be constructed at 207 Park Avenue. The early midcentury, fifty-story building on the site was landmark quality, designed by renowned architect Natalie de Blois of Skidmore, Owings & Merrill, even though the firm's male star, Gordon Bunshaft, got all the credit. It was first known as Union Carbide. In 2012, the building was renovated and environmentally upgraded to

LEED Platinum status, gaining five years of tax credits for owner JPMorgan Chase. Nevertheless, it was demolished, reportedly the world's largest voluntarily demolished building—all for eighteen additional floors! An environmental disgrace, among other things.

23. A subdistrict of the Midtown zoning district that encouraged the shift of development from the east side to the west side. "Theater District," Preservation History Database, New York Preservation Archive Project, www.nypap.org/preservation-history/theater-district/.

24. David W. Dunlap, "Developer Agrees to Plan to Cut 12 Floors From a Too-Tall Tower," *New York Times*, April 23, 1991.

25. The buildings were designed as ordinary tenements, with the Gothic facade added to match the church.

26. Hunt was the first American architect to attend L'École des Beaux Arts in Paris. He returned to design many houses for the wealthy, including the Breakers in Newport and the Biltmore estate in North Carolina.

27. The first group met over dinner at my apartment and included Victor and Sarah Kovner, Arlene and Bruce Simon, Ann and Paul Sperry, my husband, Donald, and me. Architect Steve Robinson was part of the group but couldn't attend the dinner.

## Chapter 6: A Green Thumb

1. Eventually, the Park Association became the Parks Council and now New Yorkers for Parks.

2. Caro, *Power Broker*, 510.

3. Casitas are small houses, usually one room set on an empty lot, that serve as community centers.

4. James Trainor, *Steal This Playground: New York City and the Radical Playground Movement, 1961–1976* (New York: Metropolis Books, 2017).

5. The Council on the Environment is now GrowNYC.

6. In 1975, a *New York Daily News* front-page headline, "FORD TO CITY: DROP DEAD," reflected the rejection by the federal government of financial help during the height of the city's crises.

7. See Roberta Brandes Gratz, "Bryant Park: A Model Public Space," in *Cities Back From the Edge: New Life for Downtown* (Hoboken, NJ: Wiley, 1998) 38–42.

8. Elizabeth Barlow, "32 Ways Your Time or Money Can Rescue Central Park," *New York Magazine*, June 14, 1976, 32–39.

9. Elizabeth Barlow, "Readers Respond to Park's Plight," *New York Magazine*, August 2, 1976, 6.

10. Gordon Davis is now a partner at Venable LLP.

11. A year earlier, the Vincent Astor Foundation had made a $2,500 grant to assist the association's efforts to preserve the bungalows. In 1993, the New York Foundation gave $30,000 to support the organization for three years. The Astor and New York Foundations often funded some of the same efforts as the Fund.

12. This dune area is also a designated endangered species nesting ground for the piping plover and other endangered birds.

13. For an excellent take on the problems and negative impacts of "credentialism," see Jane Jacobs, *Dark Age Ahead* (New York: Random House, 2004), a book amazingly prescient about the current times.

14. Caro, *Power Broker*, 850.

15. For a largely underappreciated story of the rebirth of the South Bronx, see Gratz, *The Living City*.

16. The family property was donated to the Long Island Nature Conservancy, and the home is now the organization's headquarters.

17. Land trusts are private, nongovernmental charities that permanently conserve land and other natural resources by acquiring land or buying conservation easements that remove potential nonconforming development.

18. The Land Trust Alliance was started by the Fund under the Rural New York program.

19. Richard Kaplan died January 21, 2016.

20. Details can be found on the museum website. Carol Willis and Mary Beth Betts, "Heritage Trails," Heritage Trails New York, Skyscraper Museum, http://skyscraper.org/heritagetrails/archive.html.

## Chapter 7: Storm King, the River, and the Hudson Valley

1. "The project involved cutting away part of the mountain, constructing a huge complex of turbines, transformers, and generators, and stringing high-tension wires across the river. Con Edison's plan was to pump millions of gallons of water during off-peak hours through a two-mile pipe from the Hudson River into the town of Cornwall's reservoir, which lay behind Storm King. During times of peak power generation, the giant utility would release the water through a forty-foot-wide tunnel inside the mountain to turn the plant's turbines. The water would then empty back into the Hudson." John H. Adams and Patricia Adams, *A Force for Nature: The Story of NRDC and the Fight to Save Our Planet* (San Francisco: Chronicle Books, 2010), 17.

2. Until then, one had to own property and show damages to that property to qualify.

3. Adams and Adams, *Force for Nature*, 17.

4. Adams and Adams, *Force for Nature*, 17.

5. Adams and Adams, *Force for Nature*, 18.

6. Klara Sauer became executive director in 1979. Scenic Hudson, together with the Wallace Fund, protected 14,500 acres of awe-inspiring landscapes and created nineteen parks for public enjoyment. Sauer also initiated Scenic Hudson's farmland-protection program and was instrumental in establishing the Hudson River Valley Greenway, covering 154 miles of the river and twelve counties, and securing congressional designation of the valley as the Maurice D. Hinchey Hudson River Valley National Heritage Area. Also during her captaining of Scenic Hudson, the group led efforts with allies to get General Electric to clean up toxic PCBs it had dumped in the Hudson River. That cleanup finally began in May 2009.

7. Al Butzel, lead attorney in the lawsuit, pointed out, "An artist's rendering in Con Edison's 1962 Annual Report sent to its shareholders in April 1963 showed the side of the Mountain cut away, leaving a gash the size of three football fields laid end-on-end with a high cliff behind. It was this illustration, in particular, that roused lovers of the Highlands to action."

8. David S. Sampson, "The Hudson River Valley Greenway and Beyond: How a Word Can Change the Way We Think About Our Land," *Proceedings of the Fábos Conference on Landscape and Greenway Planning* 4, no. 1 (2013).

9. This was the first Riverkeeper. It started a worldwide movement, and now there are hundreds of them not necessarily affiliated with each other.

10. *America's First River: Bill Moyers on the Hudson*, episode 1, "Stories From the Hudson," by Bill Moyers, aired April 23, 2002.

11. Great-grandson of famous abolitionist William Lloyd Garrison.

12. A Rifkind family member reported to me that Judge Rifkind had spoken with great pride about taking on this case.

13. Al Butzel, "Storm King Revisited: A View From the Mountaintop," *Pace Environmental Law Review* 31, no. 1 (Winter 2014): 372–373.

14. Immensely strengthened in 1970 under Nixon after Earth Day.

15. Lyndon B. Johnson, "Annual Message to the Congress on the State of the Union," January 4, 2965, www.presidency.ucsb.edu/ws /index.php?pid=26907.

16. Church designed the house with Calvert Vaux and created an elaborate, Persian-style interior.

17. It was the US Court of Appeals for the Second Circuit, which showed great sympathy with its decision in favor of the plaintiffs, that made the difference.

18. Butzel, "Storm King Revisited," 388.

19. The Hudson River Foundation, run by Clay Hiles, supports a diverse and critical array of projects, including the tagging of striped bass, oyster restoration, and the Newtown Creek Fund.

20. NRDC was founded in 1951 in Arlington, Virginia, working on nonconfrontational issues to preserve significant natural habitats and ecological preserves around the globe.

21. Eventually, this founding group would merge with a likeminded group of Yale Law School students, all brought together at the suggestion of the Ford Foundation, which agreed to fund them generously if they combined forces.

22. The Sierra Club was founded in San Francisco in 1892 by John Muir.

23. Interview with Eric Goldstein, June 3, 2020.

24. Adams and Adams, *Force for Nature*, 91.

25. He served in that position for twenty years under six successive commissioners and then twelve years as New York State deputy commissioner for historic preservation.

26. There is no definitive record of who was on the trip, but included were Brendan Gill, Kent Barwick, Victoria Newhouse, Margot Wellington, Laurie Beckelman, Susan Henshaw Jones, Suzanne Davis, Richard Kaplan, Elizabeth Kaplan Fonseca, Pattie Sullivan, John Adams, and me.

27. Daisy was a cousin of FDR, gave him his famous black Scottish terrier Fala, traveled extensively with him during his presidency, and helped establish his library in Hyde Park. She died in the house in 1991, shortly before her one hundredth birthday. Joan knew her fairly well.

28. The Hudson River national historic landmark district is eighteen miles long and thirty-two square miles.


## Chapter 8: Toward a More Civil Society

1. In the *Berman v. Parker* decision, the US Supreme Court upheld the eminent domain power under the Fifth Amendment's takings clause: "It is within the power of the legislature to determine that the community should be beautiful as well as healthy, spacious as well as clean, well-balanced as well as carefully patrolled. . . . If those who govern the District of Columbia decide that the Nation's Capital should be beautiful as well as sanitary, there is nothing in the Fifth Amendment that stands in the way."

2. Greenwald, "J.M. Kaplan Fund," 39.

3. Kismaric helped start the Time-Life photography series and for ten years was editorial director of the Aperture Foundation, a nonprofit publisher of fine-art photography books.

4. Published in association with William Morrow, W. W. Norton, Penguin Books, and Random House.

5. Hayes's work established the fundamental legal framework for the city's responsibility for the homeless.

6. *Fiction* is a literary magazine founded in 1972 by Mark Mirsky, Donald Barthelme, and Max Frisch.

7. Edith Wharton, *A Backward Glance* (Philadelphia: Curtis Publishing Company, 1933).

8. Technically, Furthermore is a program of the J.M. Kaplan Fund.

9. Chartock is also executive publisher and project director for the *Legislative Gazette*, a weekly newspaper staffed by college intern reporters covering New York State government.

10. The real estate market was still in the doldrums.

11. A.G. Sulzberger, "Urban Center Draws Its Curtains Closed," *City Room* (blog), *New York Times*, January 14, 2010, https://cityroom.blogs.nytimes.com/2010/01/14/urban-center-draw-its-curtains-closed/.

12. The Center for Architecture (downtown on LaGuardia Place) and the Museum of the City of New York (on upper Fifth Avenue) have somewhat filled the exhibition and panel-discussion niche, and the City Club of New York has filled somewhat the advocacy and litigation role, but added all up, the public voice is considerably muted and MAS is primarily limited to the Internet and joining with other civic organizations, not leading them.

13. President of MAS from 1978 to 1979. She was the city's first director of cultural affairs under Mayor John Lindsay. In 1977, she established the Public Art Fund, merging City Walls and Public Arts Council, both of which she ran.

# INDEX

231

**Roberta Brandes Gratz** is an award-winning journalist, urban critic, lecturer, and author who has published five previous books, including most recently *We're Still Here Ya Bastards: How the People of New Orleans Rebuilt Their City* and *The Battle for Gotham: New York in the Shadow of Robert Moses and Jane Jacobs*. Her writing has also appeared in the *Nation*, the *New York Times Magazine*, the *Wall Street Journal*, and the *New York Post*. She led the Eldridge Street Project for more than twenty years, the effort to restore the 1887 synagogue on the Lower East Side and establish the Eldridge Street Museum. Gratz previously served on New York City's Landmark Preservation Commission and NYC's Sustainability Advisory Board. With Jane Jacobs, she founded The Center for the Living City. Gratz lives in New York City.

# ABOUT THE J.M. KAPLAN FUND

The J.M. Kaplan Fund was established in 1945 by Jacob M. Kaplan, whose entrepreneurial style of philanthropy has endured through three generations of family leadership, driving the Fund's work as a determined champion of social, civic, and environmental causes.

Much of the Fund's asset base came from J.M. Kaplan's sale of the Welch's grape juice company to a grape growers' cooperative. A man of imagination and courage, J.M. managed the Fund for more than three decades, contributing to projects as he saw fit. In 1977, J.M.'s oldest child, Joan Davidson, assumed the Fund's presidency, creating a grants program based largely on her own deeply held convictions in regard to the natural and built environment, the arts, civil liberties, and human rights—and her belief in the excellence of New York City and State. The two-generation co-chairmanship of Richard D. Kaplan and Betsy Davidson (1993 to 2000) expanded Joan's emphasis on human rights, while notably supporting historic preservation, the arts, and a New York City portfolio of grassroots projects for parks, libraries, and more.

In 2001, the founder's seven grandchildren—four the children of Joan Davidson and three of Elizabeth Fonseca—were entrusted with the leadership of the Fund. With Peter Davidson as chair, beginning in 2000, the Fund has worked around the world on crucial initiatives to protect global marine resources; provide site preservation and conservation training in the Mediterranean; integrate foreign-born individuals who call the United States home; support youth criminal justice reform; and lower greenhouse gas emissions, among many others. In 2015, with the launch of The J.M.K. Innovation Prize, the Fund extended its legacy of catalytic funding by supporting social entrepreneurs across America.

Today, with assets of $130 million, the Fund remains committed to early stage efforts that seek to build the social and economic fabric of communities, protect the environment, and strengthen civic culture. As a fourth Kaplan generation stands ready, the Fund still aspires to "strike a blow for small, decisive things," in the words of Joan Davidson—the upstart causes and campaigns that can make a world of difference.